INTRODUCING
ISSUES WITH
**OPPOSING
VIEWPOINTS**®

Islam

Lauri S. Friedman, *Book Editor*

Bonnie Szumski, *Publisher, Series Editor*
Helen Cothran, *Managing Editor*

GREENHAVEN PRESS
An imprint of Thomson Gale, a part of The Thomson Corporation

THOMSON
———★———™
GALE

Detroit • New York • San Francisco • San Diego • New Haven, Conn. • Waterville, Maine • London • Munich

THOMSON
*—
GALE

For more information, contact
Greenhaven Press
27500 Drake Rd.
Farmington Hills, MI 48331-3535
Or you can visit our Internet site at http://www.gale.com

LIBRARY OF CONGRESS CATALOGING-IN-PUBLICATION DATA

Islam / Lauri S. Friedman, book editor.
 p. cm. — (Introducing issues with opposing viewpoints)
  Includes bibliographical references and index.
 ISBN 0-7377-3460-4 (lib. bdg. : alk. paper)
 1. Islam—21st century. 2. Islam—Essence, genius, nature. I. Friedman, Lauri S. II. Series.
 BP161.3.I723 2006
 297—dc22

                                                                    2005052727

Contents

Chapter 3: What Does the Future Hold for Islam?

Foreword

Indulging in a wide spectrum of ideas, beliefs, and perspectives is a critical cornerstone of democracy. After all, it is often debates over differences of opinion, such as whether to legalize abortion, how to treat prisoners, or when to enact the death penalty, that shape our society and drive it forward. Such diversity of thought is frequently regarded as the hallmark of a healthy and civilized culture. As the Reverend Clifford Schutjer of the First Congregational Church in Mansfield, Ohio, declared in a 2001 sermon, "Surrounding oneself with only like-minded people, restricting what we listen to or read only to what we find agreeable is irresponsible. Refusing to entertain doubts once we make up our minds is a subtle but deadly form of arrogance." With this advice in mind, Introducing Issues with Opposing Viewpoints books aim to open readers' minds to the critically divergent views that comprise our world's most important debates.

Introducing Issues with Opposing Viewpoints simplifies for students the enormous and often overwhelming mass of material now available via print and electronic media. Collected in every volume is an array of opinions that captures the essence of a particular controversy or topic. Introducing Issues with Opposing Viewpoints books embody the spirit of nineteenth-century journalist Charles A. Dana's axiom: "Fight for your opinions, but do not believe that they contain the whole truth, or the only truth." Absorbing such contrasting opinions teaches students to analyze the strength of an argument and compare it to its opposition. From this process readers can inform and strengthen their own opinions, or be exposed to new information that will change their minds. Introducing Issues with Opposing Viewpoints is a mosaic of different voices. The authors are statesmen, pundits, academics, journalists, corporations, and ordinary people who have felt compelled to share their experiences and ideas in a public forum. Their words have been collected from newspapers, journals, books, speeches, interviews, and the Internet, the fastest growing body of opinionated material in the world.

Introducing Issues with Opposing Viewpoints shares many of the well-known features of its critically acclaimed parent series, Opposing Viewpoints. The articles are presented in a pro/con format, allowing readers to absorb divergent perspectives side by side. Active reading questions preface each viewpoint, requiring the student to approach the material thoughtfully and carefully. Useful charts, graphs, and cartoons supplement each article. A thorough introduction provides readers with crucial background on an issue. An annotated bibliography points the reader toward articles, books, and Web sites that contain additional information on the topic. An appendix of organizations to contact contains a wide variety of charities, nonprofit organizations, political groups, and private enterprises that each hold a position on the issue at hand. Finally, a comprehensive index allows readers to locate content quickly and efficiently.

Introducing Issues with Opposing Viewpoints is also significantly different from Opposing Viewpoints. As the series title implies, its presentation will help introduce students to the concept of opposing viewpoints, and learn to use this material to aid in critical writing and debate. The series' four-color, accessible format makes the books attractive and inviting to readers of all levels. In addition, each viewpoint has been carefully edited to maximize a reader's understanding of the content. Short but thorough viewpoints capture the essence of an argument. A substantial, thought-provoking essay question placed at the end of each viewpoint asks the student to further investigate the issues raised in the viewpoint, compare and contrast two authors' arguments, or consider how one might go about forming an opinion on the topic at hand. Each viewpoint contains sidebars that include at-a-glance information and handy statistics. A Facts About section located in the back of the book further supplies students with relevant facts and figures.

Following in the tradition of the Opposing Viewpoints series, Greenhaven Press continues to provide readers with invaluable exposure to the controversial issues that shape our world. As John Stuart Mill once wrote: "The only way in which a human being can make some approach to knowing the whole of a subject is by hearing what can be said about it by persons of every variety of opinion and studying all modes in which it can be looked at by every character of mind. No wise man ever acquired his wisdom in any mode but this." It is to this principle that Introducing Issues with Opposing Viewpoints books are dedicated.

Introduction

"We are all—Muslim and non-Muslim alike—facing a tremendous crisis. One and a half billion people are roaring down a highway at 150 miles an hour with no driver. Unless something happens soon, a crash is inevitable."
—Hasan Mahmud, member of the Muslim Canadian Congress

Islam is the world's fastest growing religion and its second largest—it is estimated that between 1.2 and 1.5 billion people are followers. Muslims are spread all around the world on nearly every continent. Over fifty countries have Muslim majority populations, and Muslims are found in many more areas. Although Islam is frequently associated with the Middle East, it extends far beyond that region. In fact, although 90 percent of Arabs are Muslims, less than 20 percent of the worldwide Muslim community is composed of Arabs. Muslims are Middle Eastern, European, American, African, Indian, and Asian—over 50 million Muslims live in China alone. These Muslims belong to over 150 sects of Islam. Many of these sects practice their own unique traditions, and interpretations of the Koran can vary greatly from region to region. Indeed, given the global nature of the Islamic community, Muslims practice their faith in diverse ways.

Such diversity often fuels the increasingly tense and confusing discussion of whether Islam is a religion of peace or war, a religion of rights or rights violations, a religion of oppression or a religion of the oppressed. In truth, Islam is a religion of many things, sometimes contradictory, because it is practiced by so many different people who belong to so many different cultures. An international religious community with multiple millions of adherents, at times it seems that Muslims can agree upon little more than the most basic tenets of faith. With such diversity within the *ummah* (the Arabic term for the Muslim community), "What is the true nature of Islam?" is a question asked with increasing frequency in the twenty-first century by both Muslims and non-Muslims.

With no central authority to globally officiate the tenets of Islam, individual clerics issue fatwas, or religious rulings, reflecting what they

Islam, 21%

Judaism, 0.22%

Sikhism, 0.36%

Buddhism, 6%

Chinese traditional, 6%

Christianity, 33%

Nonreligious, 16%

Hinduism, 14%

Primal-indigenous, 6%

Source: www.adherents.com, 2005. Note: Total adds up to more than 100 percent because upper bound estimates were used for each group.

consider to be Islamic or un-Islamic. However, these clerics frequently disagree on religious matters because Islam is so open to interpretation. These interpretations can range on matters as simple as how to best wash before prayers to as complex as when and how to use violence.

Indeed, the use of violence has become a central issue for many Muslim leaders since September 11, 2001. Some leaders around the world have taken pains to denounce the use of violence. They find no support for terrorism in the Koran, and declare it un-Islamic. Other clerics, however, argue that Muslims have the right to use violence to defend the community against infidel, or unbelieving, invaders. The use of terrorism as a defense has found favor in a small, yet impossible to ignore, group of Muslims.

In the summer of 2005, another horrible act of violence put this group of Muslims into the world's spotlight. On July 7, four Islamic suicide bombers detonated themselves in London's subway system and on a transit bus during the morning rush hour. Fifty-six people were killed, seven hundred were wounded, and thousands worldwide reacted with shock and terror. The London bombings sent a clear message to people around the world that an action as seemingly simple as riding a bus to work might end in violence, death, and destruction.

The London bombings marked a turning point for some Muslims, motivating many parties to firmly condemn terrorism and establish

American Muslims pray at New York's Muslim World Day parade in 1999. The number of Muslims living in the United States is estimated to be between 1.8 million and 7 million.

the use of violence as un-Islamic. The Persian Gulf Arab states of Bahrain, Kuwait, Oman, Qatar, Saudi Arabia, and the United Arab Emirates made individual and group statements condemning what they called the "criminal and terrorist" explosions. A Kuwaiti official said the attacks went against "all human norms and values." The Muslim Council of Britain's secretary general Iqbal Sacranie said, "Nothing in Islam can ever justify the evil actions of the bombers." Another council of imams from London's Regent's Park mosque declared that the killings had "absolutely no sanction in Islam" and said that the terrorists "should in no sense be regarded as martyrs." Even Hamas, the Palestinian terrorist group best known for coordinating suicide attacks against Israel, issued a statement condemning the London bombings that said, "Targeting civilians in their transport means and lives is denounced and rejected."

After the London bombings, some prominent Muslim clerics wanted to go further than denouncing the bombings and decided to issue an official religious ruling against them. Therefore, the Fiqh Council of North America, a group composed of American Muslim scholars

British Muslims show their disapproval of the terrorists who carried out the London bombings at this 2005 protest.

and clerics, issued a formal fatwa against terrorism, which firmly stated: "Targeting civilians' life and property through suicide bombings
or any other method of attack is *haram*—or forbidden. . . . We pray
for the defeat of extremism and terrorism. . . . We pray for the safety
and security of all inhabitants of our planet."

It was believed such a fatwa could serve two important purposes:
On the one hand, the declaration would show the non-Muslims of
the world that the Muslim community is serious about condemning
terror. On the other hand, the fatwa would make clear to Muslims
everywhere what values are acceptable to the Muslim community and
which are strictly outside of the faith.

Yet whether these statements would help coalesce the far flung
ummah remains to be seen. Increasingly, the *ummah* appears divided
into those who believe the use of violence is un-Islamic and those who
approve its use for what they believe are holy missions. This conflict
is deep-seated and intense: U.S. trade representative Robert Zoellick
has starkly described it as "a battle for the soul of Islam." Who will
win this battle will depend in part on how well the global Muslim
community is able to establish what is definitively Islamic and what
is un-Islamic. *Introducing Issues with Opposing Viewpoints: Islam* explores
a variety of these tensions and offers readers a look into other chal-
lenges confronting Islam in the twenty-first century.

Chapter 1

Is Islam a Religion of War or Peace?

Tensions between Muslims and other religious groups run high in places such as Jerusalem, where this Muslim man prays.

Viewpoint

1

Islam Is a Peaceful Religion

Nadeem Haq

"While the history of human rights and tolerance in the West is more recent, in Islam it started 1,400 years ago."

In the following viewpoint American Muslim Nadeem Haq uses personal experience and historical example to argue that Islam has traditionally been a religion of peace and tolerance. She states that for hundreds of years, people of many different religions have lived peacefully under Islamic rule, and cites Islam's prohibition on killing innocent civilians to show that it is a religion of tolerance and restraint. She explains that violence committed in the name of Islam does not reflect the true nature of the religion; these are the actions of a few that cannot be representative of an entire faith. She concludes that all religions have endured violent episodes, and as they are not considered violent at heart, neither should Islam.

AS YOU READ, CONSIDER THE FOLLOWING QUESTIONS:
1. According to the author, who made the very first call to Islam? How does this support the author's idea that Islam is a religion of peace?

Nadeem Haq, "Islam Promotes Peace, Not Violence and Killing," *The Buffalo News,* December 8, 2002, p. H2. Copyright © 2002 by *The Buffalo News.* All rights reserved. Reproduced by permission.

2. What are two ways in which Haq claims Muslims have been victims of violence?
3. According to the author, what was the conclusion of Marcel Boisard's book on jihad?

It greatly disturbs me as a Muslim to keep hearing and reading that Islam, one of the great monotheistic religions, teaches violence. This is the religion of my family and many friends, who are some of the most peaceful people I know. Although I have never doubted the fact that Islam is a peaceful religion, the constant propaganda makes it essential that I defend my religion.

Islam Offers Peace to All

While the history of human rights and tolerance in the West is more recent, in Islam it started 1,400 years ago. In fact, a freed black slave made the first call to prayers in Islam.

Many Muslims insist that Islam is a peaceful religion that forbids murder and violence.

Sargent. © 2001 by Universal Press Syndicate. Reproduced by permission.

People of various religions have lived peacefully in Muslim lands for centuries. Islam prohibits the killing of innocent people and the destruction of property even during the state of war. The kind treatment of civilians and prisoners of war and respect for their civilization during conflict is the rule rather than the exception in Islamic history.

In the book "Jihad: A Commitment to Universal Peace," Marcel Boisard, a non-Muslim writer, concludes that the world should follow the example of Islam in times of conflict since Islam forbids excess even during war.

Muslims Are Victims of Violence, Not Perpetrators

[In 1992] in Bosnia, hundreds of thousands of Muslims were murdered and thousands of Muslim women and children were raped by the Serb Christians in the name

A peace flag is flown at a Kurdish Muslim rally in Turkey. The Kurdish people have been the frequent targets of human rights abuses.

of ethnic cleansing. Just in the last 25 years, the number of innocent Muslims killed in various conflicts numbers in the hundreds of thousands—Afghanistan, Bosnia, Iraq and Chechnya, to mention a few.

According to a recent article in the *Washington Post,* some Christian clerics facilitated the killings while the Muslims protected the victims during the Rwanda genocide in the mid-'90s. Therefore, violent behavior is not unique to Muslims and does not represent mainstream Islam.

For the majority of the last 1,400 years, the Muslims have been the protectors of Christians and Jews and their holy places in Jerusalem. However, the Christian population of that region has declined sharply since the Israeli occupation. How can such a large population of Christians exist in Palestine for centuries if the believers of my religion are so violent?

In the latest conflict in the Middle East, the number of Palestinians killed is much larger than the number of Israelis. As a Muslim, I condemn both the suicide bombers and the Israeli army, according to the teachings of Islam and my duty as an American.

Every Religion Has Those Who Misuse It

A small minority of Muslims have used Islam as an excuse to commit crimes against innocent people. But holding Islam and Muslims collectively responsible for everything that happens in the name of Islam is like asking Jesus or Moses to take responsibility for the Crusades, the Spanish Inquisition, the deaths of millions of black slaves, the destruction of Native Americans, the genocide in Bosnia and Rwanda, the massacre of innocent Palestinians in the refugee camps of Lebanon and many other atrocities committed by some misguided believers of the Judeo-Christian tradition. . . .

I am thankful to America for many things, especially for making me a better Muslim by giving me a deeper understanding of Islam, which means peace.

EVALUATING THE AUTHORS' ARGUMENTS:

In this viewpoint, Nadeem Haq argues that Islam is a religion of peace. In the following viewpoint, Abdul Maseeh argues that Islam is a religion of violence. After reading both viewpoints, what is your opinion on whether Islam is peaceful or violent? Explain.

Islam Is a Violent Religion

Abdul Maseeh

"Islam is committed to war."

In the following viewpoint Abdul Maseeh argues that Islam is a religion of violence. To support his view he cites verses from the Koran (or Qur'an), the Muslim holy book, that give permission to Muslims to kill both those who refuse to convert to Islam and those who choose to renounce Islam. Maseeh further argues that Islam is a religion that is committed to war; he cites information that shows that as of October 2001, twenty-eight of the thirty wars underway in the world involved Muslims. He concludes that the Islamic belief that Muslims should force non-believers to submit to Islam ensures that there will always be war in the world.

Abdul Maseeh is a writer who lives in the Muslim world.

AS YOU READ, CONSIDER THE FOLLOWING QUESTIONS:
1. According to the author, examples of what can be found in Chad, Indonesia, and Egypt?
2. What does sura 4, verse 89, of the Qur'an say?
3. What is the meaning of *Dar-al-Islam?*

Abdul Maseeh, "The Islamic Concept of Peace: Can the West Accept It?" *Free Inquiry,* Spring 2002, p. 39. Copyright © 2002 by the Council for Democratic and Secular Humanism, Inc. Reproduced by permission.

After much research and reflection, I have come to understand the Islamic concept of peace as something like this: Peace comes through submission, which is the meaning of the word *Islam.* This submission, of course, is submission to Muhammad and his concept of Allah in the Qur'an, in other words, Islam once again.

Accept Islam or Be Killed

Theoretically peace exists inside *Dar-al-Islam,* the House of Submission. I say "theoretically" because we all know that Muslims,

Some Muslims, such as this Pakistani man, see Osama bin Laden as an Islamic hero because bin Laden opposes the United States.

even though they are not supposed to, do fight fellow Muslims. Consider the Afghan civil war between the Pashtuns on one side and the then-Northern Alliance (Uzbeks, Tajiks, etc.) on the other; Iraq's attack on Kuwait and its earlier war with Iran; or the West Pakistan attack on East Pakistan, which subsequently became Bangladesh.

Peace with pagans, that is, people not "of the Book," is impossible; they are all to be given a chance to accept Islam or be killed. This is illustrated by the killing of pagans in the south of Sudan, the north of Nigeria, and the south of Chad, in each case by Muslims eager to impose Islamic law.

With regard to Christians and Jews, they too are to be fought against until they are subdued and feel themselves subdued—that is found in

Demonstrations in the Palestinian territories frequently involve young Muslims dressed like this man, marching with a Qur'an and a knife on the streets of the Gaza Strip.

Islamic militants burn President George W. Bush in effigy during a violent demonstration in the West Bank.

Qur'an sura 9, verse 29 ("Fight those who believe not in Allah nor the Last Day, nor hold that forbidden which hath been forbidden by Allah and His Messenger; nor acknowledge the Religion of Truth, from among the People of the Book, until they pay the *Jizya* with willing submission, and feel themselves subdued"). Examples of this are also found in Sudan, Nigeria, and Chad, and also in Indonesia—along with smaller atrocities against Christians in Egypt and the heinous repression of all Christian activity in Saudi Arabia by the Wahhabis.

Islam Is Committed to War

To say that Islam is a religion of peace is not true. Islam is committed to war, both by the example of Muhammad, who fought on until he subdued Mecca and then other tribes, and by the Qur'an's teaching supported by numerous passages in the *Hadith*. According to Amir Tahiri, editor of *Politique International* in Paris, of the thirty wars going on as of October 2001, twenty-eight involve Muslims fighting either non-Muslims or even other Muslims! The Qur'an does teach that Muslims are never to initiate war. But Islam has a strange way of putting this into practice. For example, Muslims are supposed to offer non-Muslims an opportunity to embrace Islam. If the non-Muslims refuse, this is viewed as aggression against Allah and Islam. Therefore Muslims are allowed to fight these "aggressors" until they are converted or killed.

Perhaps the greatest proof that Islam is not a religion of peace is sura 4, verse 89, which proclaims that any who want to leave Islam (turn renegade) shall be put to death: "But if they turn renegades, seize them and slay them wherever ye find them." This makes Islam the religion of fear, not of peace.

There will be war in the world as long as people believe in Muhammad, his example, and his teaching. The Islamic concept of peace, meaning making the whole world Muslim, is actually a mandate for war.

EVALUATING THE AUTHORS' ARGUMENTS:

In this viewpoint, Abdul Maseeh cites the fact that Muslims have been involved in many wars to support his argument that Islam is a violent religion. In the previous viewpoint, author Nadeem Haq agrees that Muslims have been involved in many conflicts, but portrays them as the victims of violence rather than the perpetrators. After reading both viewpoints, what is your opinion of Islam and violence? Do you see Muslims more as perpetrators of violence, as victims of it, or neither? Explain your answer.

Islamic Fundamentalism Inspires Terrorism

Lee Kuan Yew

"Muslims must counter the terrorist ideology that is based on a perverted interpretation of Islam."

In the following viewpoint, Lee Kuan Yew describes how the actions of Islamic terrorists are rooted in their religious beliefs. He discusses how a form of fundamentalist Islam called Wahhabism was the basis for the October 2002 bombing of a nightclub in Indonesia, the attack on the UN headquarters in Baghdad in August 2003, and other attacks. Followers of fundamentalist Islam, he says, believe they are fighting to the death in order to win a battle between good and evil and to establish an Islamic state in the world. He argues that these fundamentalists are taught a deviant form of Islam that encourages them to murder themselves and others in pursuit of this goal. The author urges moderate Muslims around the world to rein in extremist practitioners of their faith.

Lee Kuan Yew, a senior minister of Singapore, writes regularly for *Forbes Magazine,* from which this viewpoint was taken.

AS YOU READ, CONSIDER THE FOLLOWING QUESTIONS:
1. According to the author, what do Islamic terrorists believe they will receive for sacrificing their lives in terrorist attacks?
2. How many people were killed in the October 12, 2002, bombing of a Bali nightclub?
3. Why did convicted terrorist Imam Samudra thank the prosecution team who demanded he receive the death sentence?

S uicide bombers, like the one who blew up the UN headquarters in Baghdad [on August 19, 2003], confront the world with the most cost-effective of all terrorist weapons, designed to wreak psychological and physical havoc on enemies, attempting to make them capitulate. Saboteurs who want to fight and live, such as [soldiers like] Saddam loyalists, are not difficult to defeat. But a suicide bomber fears neither capture, interrogation nor death. He needs no escape plan when he attacks high-profile, densely populated targets like Baghdad's UN HQ. He is the most powerful weapon there is for those seeking to destabilize Iraq and make it ungovernable.

FAST FACT

Almost three years after the 2002 nightclub bombing, Bali was the scene of another terrorist attack. On October 1, 2005, twenty-six people were killed when two tourist areas were targeted by suicide bombers.

"I'll Be Happy to Die a Martyr"

What makes an ordinary Muslim become a suicide bomber? The behavior of the terrorists on trial in Indonesia [for bombing a Bali nightclub] offered a glimpse into the terrorist mind. On Aug. 7 [2003] the world was treated to a bizarre court scene in Bali. Seated before a panel of five red-robed Indonesian judges, Amrozi bin Nurhasyim, 41, was found guilty of terrorism and sentenced to death by firing squad for his role in the Bali bombing on Oct. 12, 2002. He had killed 202 persons—mostly foreigners, including 88 Australians—and had injured about 350 others.

Amrozi, a member of Jemaah Islamiah (JI)—a terrorist network linked to al Qaeda—broke into a grin and punched the air, shouting, "Allahu

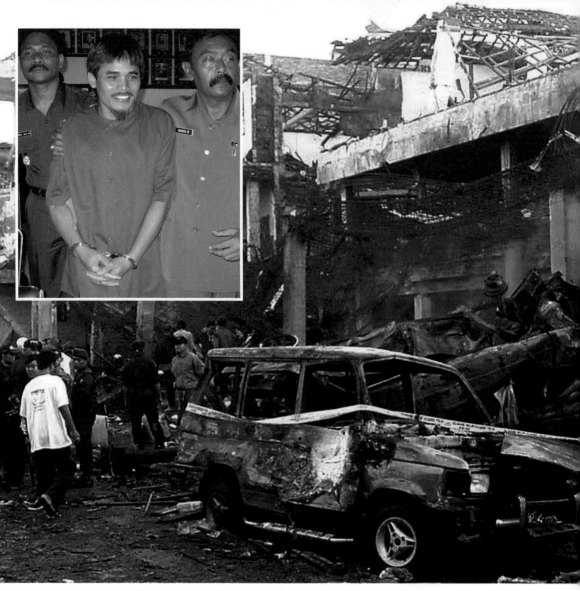

In 2003 Amrozi bin Nurhasyim (inset) was found guilty of bombing this Bali nightclub on October 12, 2002.

Akbar" ("God is great"). He then turned to face the survivors and families of those he'd killed, flashing a wide grin and giving a thumbs-up sign with both arms outstretched. "I'll be happy to die a martyr," he said. "After me, there will be a million more Amrozis."

Imam Samudra, another JI member and a mastermind of the Bali bombing, told the court that the attack was in retribution for the U.S. war on Afghanistan. "Muslims have been made scapegoats for American terrorism around the world. . . . I'd like to say thank you to the prosecution team,

The Filipino island of Mindanao, where these children live, has been ravaged by Islamic fundamentalists waging war against the government.

which has demanded the death sentence. Because in death we live peacefully, and in death we draw near to God." . . .

At the same time, in Jakarta, Abu Bakar Bashir was charged with being the spiritual head of JI and with being responsible for the bombings of several Christian churches in December 2000. He is a charismatic Muslim cleric who, through his religious schools, had recruited both Amrozi and Imam Samudra. Many terror suspects are alumni of his school. Bashir was acquitted of the serious charge of leading JI and ordering a series of attacks, but he was sentenced to four years in jail for lesser offenses. His comment: "I sell many knives, but I am not responsible for how they are used."

Sentencing the Bali bombers to death is like killing off worker bees. The queen bees—the charismatic preachers who teach a deviant form of Islam in their religious schools—will produce many more workers.

In Pursuit of a Pure Islam

When al Qaeda first infiltrated Mindanao in the southern Philippines in the late 1990s, Arab teachers had to carry out the suicide bombings. Prolonged ideological indoctrination in Wahhabi Islamism has made some Filipino Muslims believe that it is the duty of every Muslim to wage jihad; that armed struggle is the only way to bring back pure Islam and that the greatest act of devotion is to sacrifice one's life for jihad.

Now Arab fundamentalists have succeeded in twisting the teachings of Islam in Indonesia. One of the Bali bombs was set off by an Indonesian Muslim. And at Jakarta's JW Marriott Hotel bombing in August [2003], the severed head of the driver of the bomb-laden SUV was that of Asmar Latin Sani, 28, a JI member who had attended the Islamic boarding school run by Bashir. Before carrying out his mission, Sani received blessings from JI leaders to "carry out this great duty for God."

Followers of Abu Bakar Bashir (right), the head of the terrorist group Jamaah Islamiah, disguise their identities at a 2002 protest (below) in support of their leader.

Before Islam arrived—brought by Indian traders, not Arab conquerors—in the 1400s, Java had a history of many centuries of Hindu and Buddhist humanist teachings. Hence, the Javanese are the most tolerant and eclectic of Muslims. It is difficult to believe that some among them are now ready to blow themselves up in order to destroy the perceived enemies of Arab Palestinians. Psychologists who study such recruits have found that they are chosen because they are vulnerable to religious indoctrination by charismatic preachers who employ strict discipline. These preachers implant the psychology of self-sacrifice until martyrdom becomes the recruits' highest purpose in life. These followers believe that in return for their sacrifice they will become shahids ("martyrs"); that all their sins will be forgiven; and that they will have a place in shurga ("paradise"), where 72 houris ("virgins") await them.

Fighting for Control of the Muslim Soul

Governments can beef up their intelligence services, ferret out and destroy terrorist networks and harden potential targets. But only Muslims themselves—those with a moderate, more modern approach to life—can fight the fundamentalists for control of the Muslim soul. Muslims must counter the terrorist ideology that is based on a perverted interpretation of Islam. This battle will be joined when the fundamentalist Islamic terrorists seek to displace their present Muslim leaders, as they must if they are to set up their version of the Islamic state.

EVALUATING THE AUTHOR'S ARGUMENTS:

In this viewpoint, the author quotes Abu Bakar Bashir, a Muslim teacher who instructed many terrorists. In his defense, Bashir remarked, "I sell many knives, but I am not responsible for how they are used." What do you think Bashir means by this comment? Do you think that people who teach certain beliefs should be held responsible for the actions of others? Explain your reasoning.

Islamic Fundamentalist Terrorism Does Not Reflect Islam

Benazir Bhutto

"Those who would use violence and terror in the name of Islam are heretics and hypocrites."

In the following viewpoint Benazir Bhutto argues that those who claim to commit terrorism in Islam's name are not Islamic at all. She argues that terrorists ignore the most fundamental tenets of their faith that call for tolerance, peace, and kindness. If Muslims were to closely examine their faith, she believes, they would find that the Koran does not endorse many of the restrictions common in many Islamic countries today, such as repression of women, imprisonment of human rights activists, and the preaching of hate. The author counts the Muslim faith as one of the victims of the September 11 terrorist attacks because the religion was tragically co-opted by those who wanted to use it for their own corrupt purposes.

Benazir Bhutto was prime minister of Pakistan from 1988 to 1990 and from 1993 to 1996. She is the chairperson of the Pakistan People's Party.

Benazir Bhutto, "Views on Islam," *Imprimis: The National Speech Digest of Hillsdale College,* October 2002. Reproduced by permission.

AS YOU READ, CONSIDER THE FOLLOWING QUESTIONS:
  1. According to the author, what did the September 11 terrorists hate about their victims?
  2. What is the Islamic idea of ijtihad?
  3. What are two ways in which Bhutto believes Islamic terrorists do not reflect Islam?

The microcosm of America that was destroyed on September 11—people of all races, ethnicities and religions—is everything the extremists abhor: men and women, working side by side as equals; Muslims, Christians, Jews and Hindus, together building worldwide trade and communications. America is a symbol of what can be to millions of oppressed people all over the world. America means everything to those deprived of human rights and the rule of law. America symbolizes modernity, diversity and democracy, and it is these three things which are the fanatics' worst fears.

At this time of continuing crisis, the American people and their leaders must understand that those who would use violence and terror in the name of Islam are heretics and hypocrites. They are criminals, not clerics. Their actions contradict the teachings of the Holy Prophet of Islam, who wrote, "Whenever the prophet of God sent forth a detachment, he said to it, 'Do not cheat or commit treachery, nor should you mutilate or kill children, women, or old men.'" And there is a specific prohibition in Islamic law that bans killing by stealth and targeting a defenseless victim in a way intended to cause terror in a society.

The Opposite of Islam

It grieves me that included in the list of the victims of the perfidy of September 11 is the image of Islam across the world. Our religion is not what these people preach; in fact, it is the opposite. Islam is committed to tolerance and equality, and it is committed by Koranic definition to the principles of democracy. It is ironic that despite the strong commitment to democracy in Islam, most Muslims today are living in dictatorships. The Muslim people want freedom, and they need support in their search for political, economic and social empowerment. Much like the people of the communist world of the past, the Muslim people today are hostages in totalitarian regimes that flourished during the days of the Cold War.

In the West, there is often talk about the "Muslim street." The street most often seen here on television is the street of fanaticism whipped into a frenzy. But there is another Muslim street. It is a silent street of women who suffer discrimination in every aspect of life. It is a silent

Benazir Bhutto, former prime minister of Pakistan, believes that cruelty, mistreatment of women, and dictatorship have no place in Islamic belief.

street of students who are not educated. It is a silent street of business-men and businesswomen who are not allowed to compete freely. It is a silent street of human rights activists who are jailed, political parties that are decimated, and political leaders who are either prisoners or exiles. It is the street of the people constrained by the totalitarian powers of the state. It is the street of the future in the chains of present-day intolerance, ignorance and dictatorship. And it is the street far more likely to explode than the street of the religious extremists.

As I said, in Islam, dictatorship is never condoned. Nor is cruelty. In fact, according to Islam, those who commit cruel acts are condemned to destruction. Irrespective of the ignorance reflected in the actions of fanatics, there are three key princples in Islam that point

Indian Muslims protest an October 29, 2005, bombing in New Dehli by Pakistani Muslims. The posters, written in Hindi, read "Islam is a religion of peace."

Muslim women in Germany take part in a 2004 demonstration against the use of violence in the name of Islam. Their signs read "Islam is for the people" and "Islam is peace."

to democracy: consultation, known as shura; consensus, known as ijmaa; and independent judgement, known as ijtihad. Today the Muslim people are searching for freedoms that exist in other parts of the world. They are searching for forms of government that are representative and accountable. Just as Christians and Jews have the Bible to guide them, Muslims have the holy Koran. The Koran makes it clear that the principal operations of the democratic process—consultation between elected officials and the people and accountability of leaders to the people—are fundamental to Islam. The holy Koran says that Islamic society is contingent on mutual advice, through mutual discussions, on an equal footing. Consultation under the Koran demands that public decisions are made by representative officials. Consensus provides the basis for majority rule. And according to Muslim scholars, the legitimacy of the state depends upon the extent to which state organization and power reflect the will of the Muslim people.

The Enemies of Humanity

Now this is the exact opposite of the fanatical, ignorant message that is spread by [Osama] bin Laden, the Taliban and their allies in hate. These despots are the enemies of all civilizations. The terrorists who attacked America were not fighting for Islam. They were fighting for themselves. Their goal is to establish interlinked theocracies of ignorance that they can control for their own political ends. They are the enemies of Western principles, and they are the enemies of all humanity. In the end, they will be defeated.

> **EVALUATING THE AUTHOR'S ARGUMENTS:**
>
> In the viewpoint you just read, author Benazir Bhutto describes how democracy, tolerance, and equality are important characteristics of Islam. Yet she also describes how these features are rarely seen in Muslim societies. Considering what you know on this subject, how might you go about explaining this inconsistency?

American Muslims Threaten the United States

Srdja Trifkovic

"Nearly all terrorists of concern to America's national security . . . have been Muslims."

In the following viewpoint, author Srdja Trifkovic argues that the growing Muslim population in the United States represents a threat to national security. He believes out of all immigrant groups, Muslims have the least loyalty to the United States, and thus cannot be trusted to be good citizens or act in the best interest of the country. He warns that countering terrorism will be impossible until the United States recognizes the internal threat posed by its Muslim population and takes steps to monitor their activity, prevent their immigration, and curb their ability to preach radical Islam.

Srdja Trifkovic is the foreign-affairs editor of *Chronicles* and director of the Rockford Institute's Center for International Affairs.

AS YOU READ, CONSIDER THE FOLLOWING QUESTIONS:

1. According to the viewpoint, what were the findings of a survey of newly naturalized Muslim citizens?

2. In the author's opinion, why should those affiliated with Islam be barred from holding security clearance?
3. Why does the author suggest Islamic centers become registered with the attorney general?

A
l Qaeda and its loosely linked offshoots are diversifying their range of possible targets to include vital infrastructure and energy installations in the West. They are also fielding a new generation of recruits, many of them Muslim immigrants and their offspring in Europe and North America. The decentralized pattern makes countermeasures difficult, especially with self-motivated young people deeply embedded in Western host societies—such as the five young U.S.-born Yemenis from upstate New York convicted [in 2003] of plotting terrorist attacks, or the eight U.K.-born British citizens of Pakistani descent charged [in 2003] with plotting attacks on financial institutions in the United States.

It is alarming that the political class in the United States remains unwilling to examine the implications of the existence of a large Muslim diaspora in the country. Law-enforcement and intelligence professionals privately admit that the existence of that multimillion-man presence is essential in providing the terrorists with the recruits, the infrastructure, the mobility, and the relative invisibility without which they would not be able to operate, but neither the September 11 Commission's final report nor a host of related statements and proposals from both ends of the duopoly have acknowledged that reality.

The Internal Threat to America Is Increasing

That there is a correlation between the presence of a Muslim population in a country and the terrorist threat to that country is a demonstrable fact. Muslims are the only group that harbors a substantial segment of individuals who share key objectives with the terrorists, even if they do not all approve of all of their methods. They are the immigrant group least likely to identify with America: In response to a survey of newly naturalized citizens, 90 percent of Muslim immigrants said that, if there were a conflict between the United States and their country of origin, they would be inclined to support their country of origin. In Detroit, 81 percent of Muslims "strongly agree" or "somewhat agree" that *sharia* should be the law of the land.

This internal threat to America is increasing. In the aftermath of September 11, various estimates of the Muslim population of the United States have been made, ranging from two to nine million. The number of mosques and Islamic centers is around 2,000 and keeps growing. The total number of mosques increased 42 percent between 1990 and 2000, compared with a 12-percent average increase among evangelical Protestant denominations and a two-percent average increase among old-line Protestant, Roman Catholic, and Orthodox groups.

Immigration into the United States from the Middle East—around 1.5 million now, and expected to rise to 2.5 million by 2010—is likely to be exceeded by Muslim immigration from the Indian subcontinent (Pakistan, India, Bangladesh). Currently, Muslims account for one tenth of all naturalizations, but their birthrates exceed those of any other significant immigrant group. The number of U.S.-born children under 18 with at least one parent born in the Middle East will zoom from 600,000 today to just under a million by 2010.

A long-term counterterrorist strategy is impossible as long as these trends remain undiagnosed and unchecked. The application of ideological and

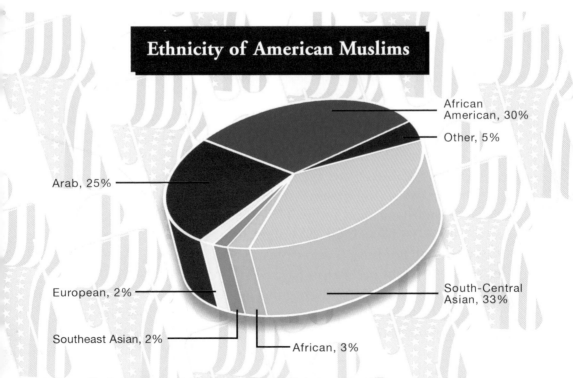

Ethnicity of American Muslims

African American, 30%
Other, 5%
Arab, 25%
European, 2%
Southeast Asian, 2%
African, 3%
South-Central Asian, 33%

Source: Hartford Institute for Religious Research, http://hirr.hartsem.edu.

political criteria in determining the eligibility of prospective visitors or immigrants has been and remains an essential ingredient of any antiterrorist strategy, and Islamic activism should be treated as eminently political, rather than "religious," activity. The problem of Muslim influx, however, is inseparable from the phenomenon of Islam itself—and, in particular, from that faith's impact on its adherents as a political ideology and a program of action. The notion that terrorism is an aberration of Islam, not a predictable consequence of the ideology of *jihad* that is inseparable from it, reflects a flawed elite consensus that must be changed. Only then can a coherent program of political and legislative action be developed to make America truly safer.

Seal the Borders and Use Profiling

The preliminary to any such effort is to seal our borders. Preventing illegal immigration is a desirable objective *per se;* in the context of stopping terrorists, it is mandatory. The means exist, the political will must be found. The September 11 Commission's final report says: "Better technology and training to detect terrorist travel documents are the most important immediate steps to reduce America's vulnerability to clandestine entry." That is incorrect. Better technology is needed, but "the most important immediate step" is controlling the borders. Knowing who is already in the country illegally, expelling them, and stopping illegal newcomers is the highest priority. State and local law-enforcement agencies should be enlisted in enforcing the law and protecting national security.

Law-enforcement agencies at all levels should be freed from the irrational ban on "profiling." Not all Muslims are terrorists, but, for some years now, nearly all terrorists of concern to America's national security and to the quality of life of her citizens have been Muslims. "The development of terrorist indicators has hardly begun," the September 11 Commission's report says, "and behavioral cues remain important." This is correct, and it is therefore time to accept that "profiling" based on a person's appearance, citizenship, origin, and apparent or suspected beliefs must be an essential tool of the trade of law enforcement and the "War on Terror."

Curb Immigration and Monitor Muslims

The essential legislative step forward would entail enacting new immigration legislation to exclude all persons engaged in Islamic activism from America. Such activism should be defined as propagating, disseminating, or otherwise supporting *jihad* (in its primary sense of divinely sanctioned war against non-Muslims); discrimination against Christians, Jews, and other "infidels"; discrimination and violence against women; the sanction of slavery, a poll tax, *etc.* Islam's violent manifestations and its discriminatory scriptural message are inseparable. Adequate safeguards against the adherents of that message must be put in place. The proposed definition of Islamic activism would be a major step in the direction of denying actual or potential terrorists a foothold on our shores. . . .

In addition, it will be necessary to mandate registration of Islamic centers and their individual members with the attorney general and to

Worshippers pray at a mosque in Dearborn, Michigan. Dearborn is home to the largest Muslim community in the United States.

subject them to the security supervision and legal limitations that apply to other cults prone to violence. All over the Western world, Islamic centers have provided platforms for exhortations to the faithful to support causes and to engage in acts that are morally reprehensible, legally punishable, and detrimental to the host country's national security. . . .

Islamic activism should be treated as grounds for the exclusion or deportation of any alien, regardless of status or ties in the United States, and for the loss of acquired U.S. citizenship and deportation. The presence in this country of any visitor, resident alien, or naturalized American who preaches *jihad,* discrimination against "infidels" and women, the establishment of *sharia, etc.,* is inherently prejudicial to the public interest, inimical to social harmony, and injurious to national security. . . .

Last, but by no means least, affiliation with Islam should be taken as grounds for denial or revoking of any level of security clearance. Such affiliation is incompatible with the requirements of personal commitment, patriotic loyalty, and unquestionable reliability that are essential in the military, law enforcement, intelligence services, and other related branches of government. The presence of practicing Muslims in any of these institutions presents an inherent risk to its integrity and undermines morale.

Acceptance of these proposals would represent a new start in devising a long-term defense against terrorism. They reflect the seriousness of the struggle. This war is being fought, on the Islamic side, with the deep conviction that the West is on its last legs. It is time to prove them wrong with truly robust measures of self-defense.

EVALUATING THE AUTHOR'S ARGUMENTS:

In this viewpoint, author Srdja Trifkovic argues that the Muslim American community should be monitored and restricted because of its potential to support terrorism. What is your opinion of this approach to national security? Explain your answer.

The United States Persecutes American Muslims

Hatem Abudayyeh, interviewed by Megan Harrington

"The Justice Department's new 'special registration' requirements target Muslim and Arab men."

Hatem Abudayyeh is the executive director of the Arab American Action Network, a Chicago-based community action organiza- tion that provides a variety of services to Arab American Muslims. In the following interview conducted by writer Megan Harrington, Abudayyeh describes the heightened scrutiny of Arab Americans since the terrorist attacks of September 11. He claims the Arab American community has been unfairly subject to feder- al investigation, deportation, physical violence, and discrimination. Moreover, such thorough scrutiny has not provided any evidence of links to terrorism. The author laments that America's Arab Muslims must undergo such racism and prejudice in the name of national security.

AS YOU READ, CONSIDER THE FOLLOWING QUESTIONS:

1. According to the author, in what way have Arab and Muslim students been targeted by the government?

Megan Harrington, "Arab and Muslim Immigrants Under Fire: Interview with Hatem Abudayyeh of the Arab American Action Network," *Dollars & Sense,* no. 248, July/August 2003, pp. 16–18. Copyright © 2003 by Economic Affairs Bureau, Inc. Reproduced by permission of *Dollars & Sense,* a progressive economics magazine, www.dollarsandsense.org.

2. What are voluntary interviews?

3. According to Abudayyeh, how many Arabs and Muslims are being held in detention?

Q : *In what new ways has the U.S. government targeted Arabs and Muslims for oppression and discrimination since September 11 and the war in Iraq?*

ABUDAYYEH: Starting with the USA Patriot Act, draconian measures and indiscriminate detentions and deportations have destabilized and crimininalized Arab communities across the United States. [The USA Patriot Act, passed by Congress six weeks after September 11, expands the government's authority to spy on its own citizens and permits detention and deportation of noncitizens suspected of supporting groups the government considers "terrorist" organizations.—*Eds.*] Also since September 11, U.S.-based Arab and Islamic organizations that provide humanitarian assistance to the people of war-torn nations including Palestine, Afghanistan, and Iraq have been accused of "supporting terrorism" and summarily closed down by the Justice Department. Prominent leaders have been arrested, including Rabih Haddad, co-founder of the Global Relief Foundation. Haddad has been in jail—first in Michigan, now in Illinois—since December 2001. Neither he nor the other detainees have been officially charged with any crime.

The Justice Department's new "special registration" requirements target Muslim and Arab men. In addition, the FBI has conducted around 5,000 "voluntary interviews" throughout Arab and Muslim communities. Since the war in Iraq began, still more Iraqis were called in for "voluntary" interviews.

Q: What are these voluntary interviews and have they led to arrests?

ABUDAYYEH: We know from discussions with the National Lawyers Guild that some of the questions the FBI asks relate to activism and organizing. These include "Who are the leaders of anti-war organizing in your mosques or your community centers?" and "Are there any political organizations that are functioning in your community?" Arab anti-war work, along with the anti-war movement as a whole, has been subject to the widespread "criminalization of dissent." But Arab antiwar activism is uniquely subject to aggressive state monitoring, intimidation, and threat of detention or deportation.

Exactly zero arrests related to "terrorism" have resulted from these interviews. Seventeen arrests were made altogether (for minor, technical immigration violations).

In 2002 a supporter protests on behalf of Rabih Haddad, a Lebanese citizen who helped create an Islamic charity in the United States.

Mass Detentions and Spying

Q: What has been the scale of detentions and deportations nation-wide?

ABUDAYYEH: The most accurate numbers are from the American-Arab Anti-Discrimination Committee (ADC), the Arab American Institute (AAI), and other civil rights and research groups. There was an initial round-up just after 9/11. More detentions have followed, mostly resulting from the Justice Department's new special registration requirements.

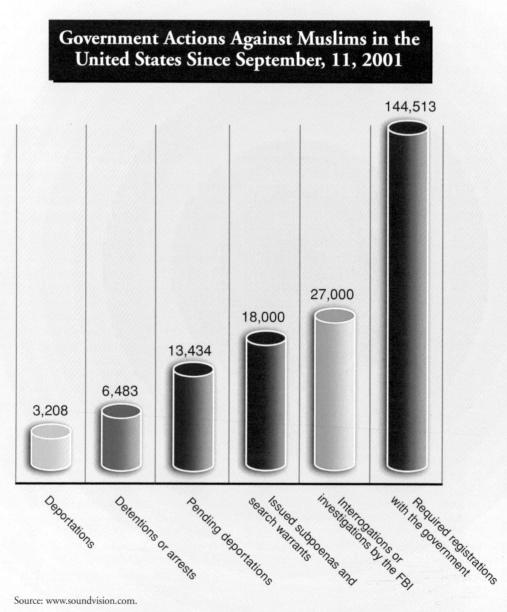

Government Actions Against Muslims in the United States Since September, 11, 2001

- Deportations: 3,208
- Detentions or arrests: 6,483
- Pending deportations: 13,434
- Issued subpoenas and search warrants: 18,000
- Interrogations or investigations by the FBI: 27,000
- Required registrations with the government: 144,513

Source: www.soundvision.com.

Over 1,200 Arabs and Muslims are still in detention today. Many thousands have been detained for various periods. Some of those were deported, but others released. Only a tiny percentage of the detainees have been charged with having any relationship with "terrorists," but even that evidence is kept secret from the defendants and their lawyers. . . .

Q: How widespread is the problem of colleges giving information on Arab students to the government?

ABUDAYYEH: Throughout the country, universities and community colleges have been providing information about their international students to the Department of Justice and the FBI. The Patriot Act expanded the government's authority to access financial and academic records of international students without their knowledge. Some universities have complied with government pressure for information, and

others have not—because of administrators' personal convictions, or because of student and faculty protests. Soon the Student and Exchange Visitor Information System (SEViS) program—which was authorized through an earlier piece of legislation—will begin tracking the 500,000-plus foreign students holding student (F-1, M-1, or J-1) visas. . . . SEViS will mostly be used to make sure that students are fulfilling the terms of their respective visas—that they're full-time students and passing their classes. But it may also require professors to monitor the activities, inside and outside the classroom, of students in certain fields of study, as well as Arab and Muslim students in other fields. It will help the government essentially "spy" on foreign students.

Meanwhile there has been an astonishing 50% drop in the U.S. government's acceptance of visitors' visa applications from Arab and Muslim countries, according to research compiled from INS [Immigration and Naturalization Service] data.

Discrimination and Racism
Q: What are the economic effects on families when a father or son is deported?

Protesters at a 2002 Seattle rally demonstrate on behalf of the Arab and Muslim immigrants who have been taken into police custody since the September 11, 2001, attacks.

ABUDAYYEH: One man who owns a restaurant on the southwest side of Chicago, and was detained for over four months, has a wife and four children. The restaurant was closed for the entire time he was detained, and his family had to apply for public aid benefits to be able to economically survive. This is a specific story, and luckily this man returned to his family and his business, but for the deported heads of household, their families have financially suffered greatly, and are reaching out to other family members, community centers, mosques, and welfare programs for assistance.

Q: Have other types of discrimination—in schools and on the street—increased?

ABUDAYYEH: We have heard anecdotally of a number of incidents in Chicago from high school students that we work with. They have been dealing with faculty and administrators that racially, ethnically, and religiously profile them in their classrooms, using broad misrepresentations of their culture and religion in ways that marginalize them.

Also, there have been racist attacks on mosques and churches, including St. John's, an Assyrian church on the far northeast side of Chicago, as well as dozens of incidents of physical attacks on Arab and Muslim men, youth, and women—especially against females who wear the traditional Muslim headdress, the *hijab*. One woman was just walking down the street with her baby in a stroller. A white male approached her, yelled something indecipherable about "Arabs" and "terrorism," and then ripped the *hijab* off of her head. . . .

Q: *What can be done in this climate?*

ABUDAYYEH: . . . It is very important to connect these anti-Arab and anti-Muslim attacks with the historical racial profiling and anti-immigrant policies of the U.S. government. A movement for true racial and social justice must include the unity of the multinational working class with the oppressed nationalities of this country.

EVALUATING THE AUTHORS' ARGUMENTS:

In this viewpoint, Hatem Abudayyeh depicts an innocent Muslim American community that has been unfairly singled out by authorities on unfounded suspicions of terrorism. In the previous viewpoint, author Srdja Trifkovic depicts a Muslim American community that threatens national security by providing a breeding ground for terrorism and anti-American sentiment. How do you think it is that these authors have such different ideas about the Muslim community in America? Do you agree with one perception more than the other? Why?

Chapter 2

Does Islam Respect Human Rights?

A woman's status under Islam is part of the debate over whether Islam respects human rights.

Islamic Law Violates Human Rights

David Finkel

"You don't amputate a sinner, you don't stone a person to death, you bring a person about by grace."

In the following viewpoint, reporter David Finkel describes the penal system in the Muslim states of Nigeria, where amputation, whipping, and stoning are acceptable punishments for crime. These punishments are derived from sharia, or Islamic law. The author describes how judges rule from law books based solely on Islam, and how defendants are routinely tortured and forced to confess to crimes they did not commit. This is done with the approval of Nigeria's leading Muslims, who seek to establish an Islamic state that is completely independent from Western values and systems. David Finkel is a staff writer for the *Washington Post,* from which this viewpoint was taken.

AS YOU READ, CONSIDER THE FOLLOWING QUESTIONS:
1. Under Nigeria's Islamic law, what is the penalty for adultery?
2. How does the Islamic leader Mujahid view the difference between justice in a democracy and justice in Islam?
3. According to the author, what is Bello Ali's predicament?

David Finkel, "Crime and Holy Punishment," *Washington Post,* November 24, 2002, p. A01. Copyright © 2002 by Washington Post Book World Service/Washington Post Writers Group. Reproduced by permission.

I n the continuing search for justice, comes now Case No. 88/2002: "Theft of Sheep and Ram."

The facts, as outlined in the court files, couldn't be more ordinary.

There was a sheep. There was a ram. They were worth about $30. They were stolen.

The trial, which has just begun, seems unexceptional as well.

"Did you steal them?" asks the judge, who sits at the front of a hot, heavy-aired, cement box of a room whose wall decorations are an out-of-date calendar, a leather bag with a copy of the Koran inside, and a whip.

"Yes," says the first defendant.

"Yes," says the second.

"Yes," says the third.

But what happens next does have significance—not only to the three defendants, but to Funtua, a town with a history of religious riots, and the state of Katsina, where a woman faces a death sentence for committing adultery, and the nation of Nigeria, where a population nervously split between Muslims and Christians reflects rising religious and ethnic tensions worldwide. It is in this context that the judge reads aloud from Katsina's penal code, which was recently rewritten to conform to the Islamic system of laws called *sharia*.

"Whoever commits the offense of theft," he says, "shall be punished with amputation of the right hand from the joint of the wrist." . . .

"I have decided to be lenient," the judge says, and with that the three are led outside, followed by everyone else in the courtroom who form a ring around a bench where the first of the three, the 13-year-old, is directed to sit.

Take off your shirt, he is told.

Now, sensing what is about to happen, dozens of passersby join the crowd as the last person emerges from the court, a man who has stopped at the wall and taken down the whip.

Crack.

In 2002 an Islamic court in Nigeria sentenced Amina Lawal to death by stoning for giving birth to a child out of wedlock.

The first lash slices across the left side of the boy's upper back. He arches in surprise as the man swings again.

Crack.

This one, harder, cuts a long mark into the boy's skin.

Crack.

Another slice. The boy, in pain, curls forward.

Crack.

"This is God's justice," one of the onlookers says approvingly.

Crack.

God's justice, then, in "Theft of Sheep and Ram":

"I felt it deep inside my flesh," the boy says after 10 lashes, and swears he will never steal again. . . .

Muslims pray in Kano, a city in Nigeria where sharia, or Islamic jurisprudence, is law.

God's Justice

For Nigeria's 50 million Christians, there are no criminal penalties for such behavior. But there are penalties for many of its 65 million Muslims, particularly those who live in Nigeria's predominantly Muslim northern states.

This is because of sharia, which, to Muslims, is a God-given code for how a life ought to be lived. Used in varying degrees, for most Muslims it is a guide to such individual activities as prayer, fasting and donating to the poor. Beyond that, many Muslim countries have adopted sharia as their civil law, governing such things as marriage and inheritance. And then there are the countries that use sharia as their criminal law, applying its judgments and penalties to such offenses as theft and adultery, which are known in sharia as Hadd offenses.

While the list of countries that use sharia as their civil law is lengthy, the list of countries that use it to judge Hadd offenses is a much smaller part of the Islamic world. There's Saudi Arabia. There's Iran. There's Sudan. Perhaps most famously, there was Afghanistan under Taliban rule. There are a few other places where criminal sharia is applied regionally, such as in parts of Pakistan. And now there's Nigeria, where Muslims in 12 of the country's 36 states find themselves facing sentences that differ greatly from the sentences handed out to the country's non-Muslims.

Theft? That's amputation of the right hand. Theft a second time? That's amputation of the left foot. An unmarried person who has sex? That's 100 lashes. A person who commits adultery? That's burial up to the waist and being pelted in the head with stones until death. . . .

Forced Confessions and Torture

The judge with the most stoning and amputation sentences since sharia's implementation [is Bawa] Tambuwal [who] can be found in the very northwestern reaches of Nigeria, in the city of Sokoto, which is the capital of Sokoto state. On his docket this day is the case of a 19-year-old defendant named Bello Ali, who is accused of theft and is waiting for his trial to begin. He is in a holding cell, head resting in hands that are unblemished except for a nickel-sized sore on the outer bone of each of the wrists. . . .

Out of earshot of the judge, he says that he didn't do it, that he was asleep in his father's car when he was suddenly dragged out, that "the police beat me up so I would confess."

He holds out his hands and exposes his wrists. This is the spot, of course, where an amputation would occur—but Ali's point is the sores.

"They hung me up using ropes."

Now he turns around, lifts his shirt, and shows a back striped with long, black marks.

"They used sticks on me."

He lowers the shirt and tries to explain why he didn't bring this up in court.

"If justice is done, I will be released," he says, but "whatever the court decides under sharia, I will accept it."

Even amputation?

He shrugs. He is a Muslim, he says. He believes in God. He believes in destiny. . . .

Allah Wants It

Mujahid is the leader of one of the largest radical Islamic groups in Nigeria, called Jaamutu Tajidmul Islami, or the Movement for Islamic Revival. A student of Nigerian history, he is well aware that the implementation of criminal sharia, which had existed in Nigeria before it was interrupted by British rule, "is not a sudden occurrence. It is something that has been boiling up." . . .

While "the sharia implementation has just started," says Mujahid, "the ultimate is to have an Islamic state, where we are not bound by the West." By "West," he means the United States, which he describes as "arrogant" and "a symbol of injustice in the world."

"What is the difference between justice in democracy and justice in Islam?" he says. "The answer is justice in democracy is because the people want it, it's the mandate of the people, but justice in Islam is that the people feel the creator, Allah, wants it. We are doing it because we are feeling this is what the creator wants us to do. In democracy, the interpretation of justice can be adapted. In Islam, it cannot."

"Don't Amputate a Sinner"

Not everyone in Zamfara agrees with Mujahid. "Sharia is a religious law, an Islamic law, but it is not a Christian law," says Linus Awuhe, explaining one reason he opposes sharia's implementation. In addition to being a priest, Awuhe is the Zamfara chairman of the Christian Association of Nigeria. "I am not saying they're not entitled to their beliefs. What I am saying is they should not force their beliefs on me.

"Secondly," he continues, "the manner in which the sharia law is implemented goes against my own fundamental human rights. When you talk of the issue of sin and punishment, you don't amputate a sinner, you don't stone a person to death, you bring a person about by grace." . . .

Mujahid, though, says that people who would agree with Awuhe are missing the point. By stoning to death an adulterer, "you stop him from committing adultery. If he lives, he goes on to commit many many more adulteries, and those result in children being born who grow up and become drunks or armed robbers who kill people." Clearly, what Nigeria needs isn't less, sharia, he says, but more.

His goal? "Justice," he says.

EVALUATING THE AUTHOR'S ARGUMENTS:

In this viewpoint, author David Finkel describes an Islamic leader named Mujahid who believes that by stoning to death an adulterer, one deters future adulterers. Do you agree with this logic? Why or why not?

Islam Condemns the Violation of Human Rights

Asghar Ali Engineer

"Any suppression of one's freedom . . . is against humanity and hence against Islam."

In the following viewpoint, author Asghar Ali Engineer argues that a true interpretation of Islam reveals that it condemns the violation of human rights. He describes the ways in which Islam stands for social justice, equality, compassion and freedom. The reason why Muslim nations experience so many violations of human rights, Engineer explains, is because they are led by corrupt dictators who have abandoned true Islam and have replaced it with radical interpretations of Islamic law. He calls on Muslims to undergo an Islamic Renaissance that would embrace true Islamic values that have been lost through the ages.

Asghar Ali Engineer is a professor and the head of the Institute for Islamic Studies in Bombay, India.

AS YOU READ, CONSIDER THE FOLLOWING QUESTIONS:
1. According to the author, what is the Islamic value of rahmah?
2. In Engineer's opinion, what are some of the duties of a mu'min, an engaged Muslim?
3. What did the Prophet Muhammad do when his followers went against his practices, according to the author?

Asghar Ali Engineer, "Engaged Islam," *Islam and Modern Age,* www.csss-isla.com, May 2003. Reproduced by permission.

It seems the very spirit of Islam has been lost the way Muslims behave. The orthodox 'ulama insists, in Muslim majority states, to implement Shari'ah laws as they are and even insists on stoning adulterers to death. This is so from Indonesia to Algeria. There are very few Muslim states, which can be termed as liberal and democratic. Millions of Muslims are suffering as a result of this, particularly women. In countries like Kuwait women cannot vote, in countries like Saudi Arabia they cannot go out alone, Taliban [in Afghanistan] did not allow them to go to schools and in most of the Muslim countries they have to wrap themselves into [a] veil. In Saudi Arabia recently when a girls school caught fire, some girls tried to escape but were pushed back to burn alive simply because they had left their veil behind in a rush. Thus human life has no value. . . .

True Islam Promotes Equality and Human Rights

These are such matters that Muslims have to reflect deeply about and engage themselves in the serious project of changing society so as to be more progressive in keeping with Islamic values. A Muslim is, above all, [a] believer in these values. Islam had conceived of [the] emergence of a new man—a mu'min—who firmly believed in Islamic values and engaged himself in changing the world in accordance with those values.

First, I would like to throw some light on these Islamic values. The most fundamental Islamic value is justice (*'adl*) and Allah's name is 'Aadil, i.e., Just. Allah is Just. A Muslim cannot be a Muslim without being just. He has to engage himself in promoting justice in the whole world.

Another important Qur'anic value is *ihsan*—benevolence, doing good to others, and Allah's name is Muhsin, i.e., Benevolent. Allah is [the] benefactor of one and all without any distinction of caste, creed or colour. A Muslim also has to be [the] benefactor of all—Muslim or non-Muslim. The Prophet [Muhammad] has also said that a hand of a mu'min should not do any harm to the other.

Another significant Islamic value is equality. All human beings are equal inasmuch as we share our humanity with each other. All children of Adam, according to the Qur'an (17:70) possess honour and dignity accorded by Allah. This is to be seen in conjunction with freedom of conscience (2:256). One cannot think of human dignity without the concept of freedom of conscience. Thus equality, human dignity and freedom of conscience all are related with each other and cannot be compromised in any way. A society which is Islamic in [a] substantial way must ensure all three to all human beings.

Yet another important value is compassion, called in the Qur'an as *rahmah*. Allah is called Rahim, Compassionate. He is also referred to as Rahman which means almost the same, i.e., compassionate, though the Muslim theologians make some fine distinctions between the two. Rahman, according to the theologians is Allah's attribute of Mercy for all, whatever the caste, creed or nationality. Thus a Muslim must display compassion for all and should be extremely sensitive to others' suffering. A Muslim cannot be indifferent to [the] suffering of others, including animals.

A mu'min should also strive continuously for removing suffering from earth. . . . A Muslim must dedicate himself to removal of suffering in all its forms from this earth. And any form of injustice causes suffering and hence establishment of justice is directly related to removal of suffering from earth. The Qur'an repeatedly condemns oppression and exploitation, what it calls *zulm*. . . .

Afghan women under the Taliban were required to veil themselves from head to toe.

True Muslims Must Fight Injustice and Oppression

Thus an engaged Muslim must devote himself to fighting *zulm*, i.e., any form of injustice and oppression on earth. He should help all those who are victims of injustice. According to the Qur'an Moses actively helped the Israelites throw away the bondage of Pharaoh. He rid them of the oppression and exploitation and gave them [a] sense of dignity and honour as free people.

In our own times we have various forms of oppression and exploitation, be it capitalist exploitation, be it due to globalization or be it due to any other form of injustice between two individuals or between two nations or communities.

A real jihad for a Muslim is to fight against all forms of injustices and all forms of exploitation and make all forms of sacrifices to remove these injustices to establish real peace on earth. As long as there is any trace of injustice and exploitation on earth there will be violence in some form or the other and it is [the] duty of a mu'min to wage [a] struggle to remove all traces of injustice. An engaged Muslim has to be committed to peace on earth, and without peace this earth will not be worth inhabiting for all human beings. . . .

Iraqi women march for women's rights in 2005. Fighting against injustice and oppression is one way to wage jihad.

Muslim women in Afghanistan attend a presidential election rally. In doing so, they embrace what some believe is the true democratic quality of Islam.

Islam Supports Democracy and Human Rights

Unfortunately most of the people think that there is no democracy in the Islamic world because Islam is against democracy and supports authoritarianism and opposes any progress and change.

This is far from true. Islam has never approved of monarchy or authoritarianism. Monarchy developed in Islam under the influence of feudalism and under the influence of [the] Roman and Sassanid empires, not because of Islamic teachings. In fact The Holy Prophet was not followed by any monarch but by a Khalifa [caliph, or Islamic ruler] elected by the Muslims (according to Sunni Muslims) or by Imamat (according to the Shi'ah Islam). Authoritarianism has no place at all in Islamic teachings. . . .

Submission to authoritarian rule itself is un-Islamic. [The] right to open criticism is a sacred right, not because the western democracies approve it but in the earliest Islamic period the Prophet's successors accepted it. The Prophet himself never discouraged any of his followers to ask him questions even when they went against some of his practices. . . .

Thus freedom of conscience . . . is a sacred freedom, which every Muslim should guard jealously and promote fearlessly. Thus a true Muslim should be strongly committed to democratic values and should refuse to accept any authoritarian regime be it in the field of religion or in the field of politics. . . .

Similarly a true Muslim must be as much committed to the concept of human rights, as this concept is very closely related to democratic rights. The greatest violation of human rights takes place in authoritarian regimes. . . .

The Muslim World Has Deviated from Islam

Any suppression of one's freedom, be it physical or spritual, is against humanity and hence against Islam. In [the] Islamic world today we see great violations of human rights. In fact the Islamic world should have been [the] precursor in the field of democratic and human rights. But historically the Muslim world deviated from the Qur'anic teachings and, under the alien influence of medievalism, it discarded Qur'anic teachings and took to authoritarian culture. The popular aspirations and democratic rights are being crushed by the authorities. It is much more so in [the] case of women. They do not enjoy even [the] right to vote in some countries like Kuwait in the name of Islam.

Thus those committed to democratic and human rights have to fight against very heavy odds, but fight they must under inspiration from the Qur'anic culture of openness and freedom. This has long been lost through the ages. It needs to be revived. It would be [a] real Islamic renaissance.

EVALUATING THE AUTHORS' ARGUMENTS:

In the previous viewpoint, author David Finkel describes how the Muslim states of Nigeria use Islamic law to violate human rights. In this viewpoint, author Asghar Ali Engineer argues that Islam has been misinterpreted by those who use it to violate human rights. After reading both viewpoints, what is your opinion on the true nature of Islam? Do you find the explanation that Islam has been misinterpreted plausible? Explain your answer.

Islam Oppresses Women

Azam Kamguian

"The rise of political Islam has rolled back women's rights and impoverished their lives."

In the following viewpoint, Middle Eastern feminist Azam Kamguian argues that Islam oppresses women throughout the Middle East. She describes how sharia, or Islamic law, decrees that women are to be denied access to education, health care, and the basic rights associated with citizenship. As second-class citizens in many Islamic countries, women cannot vote, inherit property, be employed in a wide range of professions, or receive protection from rape, domestic violence, and honor killings. Although some apologists seek to disassociate Islam with the repressions imposed by these governments, the author argues that because all base their oppressive laws on the sharia, the oppression exists within Islam. Kamguian believes that Middle Eastern women can only be liberated if Islam is no longer used to determine the laws of the state.

Azam Kamguian is an activist and writer who deals with issues affecting women in the Middle East.

Azam Kamguian, "Islam and the Liberation of Women in the Middle East: Separation of Mosque and State Is the Only Answer," *Free Inquiry,* vol. 23, October/November 2003. Copyright © 2003 by Council for Democratic and Secular Humanism, Inc. Reproduced by permission.

AS YOU READ, CONSIDER THE FOLLOWING QUESTIONS:
  1. Why does the author believe it is useless to reform Islam?
  2. Women in many Arab countries must obtain permission from a male to do certain activities. What are they?
  3. According to the author, when did the political Islam movement begin to spread?

Women's status in Middle Eastern societies has aroused great interest recently. What role do Islamic ideology and practice play in the oppression of women in the region and other societies where Islam holds sway?

Few would argue that the situation of Middle Eastern women can be understood without reference to Islam. Although no two Middle Eastern countries have identical legal-religious systems, women are second-class citizens in all of them. But the position of women in the region cannot be understood without a thorough appreciation of the economic and political contexts in which they live, in addition to Islam's long-standing influence.

Avoiding the Truth

There are many schools of thought in this debate. One group denies that the great majority of women are any more oppressed than are non–Middle Eastern women. A second group says that oppression is real but extrinsic to Islam and the Qur'an—which, they say, intended gender equality but has been undermined by Arabic patriarchy and foreign influence.

Among intellectuals and in the academic world, any attempt to blame Islam for women's oppression is stamped as Orientalism. Those who defend Islam against Western critiques focus on proving the "progressive" nature of the Qur'an, Hadith, and Sharia, either by denying the low status of women in Middle Eastern societies, or by attributing it to pre-Islamic traditions and the contemporary political Islamic movement.

Many feminists and academic intellectuals apologize for Islam by saying that such practices as veiling women and female genital mutilation are not restricted to Middle Eastern societies. Some say that women who wear make-up in the West are just as oppressed, but it is a Postmodernist, neo-colonialist kind of oppression. They say that all religions regard women as inferior. . . .

[Yet] if Islam has no effect on women's status, why is the position of women in the Middle East worse than in any other part of the world? . . .

Islam Has Rolled Back Women's Rights

In recent decades the rise of political Islam has rolled back women's rights and impoverished their lives across the region. Political Islam as a political movement arose in reaction to secular and progressive

Many women in Pakistan, where this demonstration was staged, do not enjoy the same rights as men, such as the right to a fair trial or access to medical care.

liberation movements, which had heightened egalitarianism and brought about cultural and intellectual advances. The political Islamic movement started to gather real power and to spread in the 1970s. During the 1980s it was supported and nurtured by Western governments, which found it useful in Cold War conflicts and in opposing progressive movements in the region. Key features of political Islam included opposition to women's freedom and civil liberties, and to their freedom of expression in the cultural and personal domains. It supports the enforcement of brutal laws and traditions, including beheading and genocide. In Iran, the Sudan, Pakistan, and Afghanistan under the Taliban, Islamic regimes transformed societies in general and women's homes in particular into prisons. For women, confinement, exclusion from many fields of work and education, and brutal treatment became the law of the land. In addition, the misogynist rhetoric of political Islam in the social sphere implicitly sanctioned male violence towards women.

At present, women throughout the region are second-class citizens, being excluded from the rights, privileges, and security that all citizens of a country should enjoy. Unjust laws, discriminatory constitu-

Payne. © 2002 by *Detroit News*. Reproduced by permission of United Feature Syndicate, Inc.

tions, and biased mentalities that do not recognize women as equal citizens violate women's rights. A national, that is, a citizen, is defined as someone who is a native or naturalized member of a state. A national is entitled to the rights and privileges allotted to a free individual and to protection from the state. However, in no country in the Middle East or Northern Africa are women granted full citizenship: in every country they are second-class citizens. In many cases, the laws and codes of the state work to reinforce gender inequality and exclusion from nationality. The state is used to strengthen Islamic and tribal/familial control over women, making them even more dependent on these institutions. Unlike in the West, where the individual is the basic unit of the state, it is the family that is the basis of Arab states. This means that the state is primarily concerned with the protection of the family rather than the protection of the family's individual members. Within this framework, the rights of women are expressed solely in their roles as wives and mothers. State discrimination against women in the family is expressed through, among other things, unjust family laws that deny women equal access to divorce and child custody.

FAST FACT

Honor killings are an ancient Muslim tradition in which a male member of a family is allowed to kill a female relative if she tarnishes the family image. Honor killings occur today in the Sudan, Egypt, Iran, Iraq, Lebanon, Jordan, Morocco, Saudi Arabia, Syria, Afghanistan, and Pakistan.

The Plight of Arab Women

Throughout the region, Arab women who marry foreigners are denied the right to extend citizenship to their husbands. Furthermore only fathers, not mothers, can independently pass citizenship to their children. In many cases, where a woman has been widowed, divorced, or abandoned, or if her husband is not a national in the country where the couple reside, her children have no access to citizenship or its rights. These rights include access to education, health care, land ownership, and inheritance. There is no such obstacle to men who wish to extend their nationality to their wives and children. This inequality not only

Professor Mohja Kahf founded a Muslim feminist group called Daughters of Hajar, which works to advance the position of women under Islam.

denies women their right as citizens; it also denies children their basic rights as human beings.

If the law is designed to protect women only within their role in the family, it will fail to protect those who need protection from their families. By failing to protect women from violence such as domestic abuse, rape, marital rape, and honor killing, the state fails to provide the rights available to a full citizen. In fact, by ignoring issues of gender-based violence and granting lenient punishments to the perpetrators of violence against women, the state actually reinforces women's exclusion from the rights of citizens.

Family laws based on Sharia frequently require women to obtain a male relative's permission to undertake activities that should be theirs by right. This increases the dependency women have on their male family members in economic, social, and legal matters. For example, in many Arab countries adult women must obtain the permission of their fathers, brothers, or husbands in order to attain a passport, travel outside of their country, start a business, receive a bank loan, open a bank account, or get married.

Islam Must Be Caged

Given Islam's intrinsic animosity to equality between the sexes, to women's rights, and toward women's roles in society, how can the condition of women in Islamic societies be improved? The answer must be to eliminate political Islam as a precondition to any improvements in the status of women in the Middle East. The social system is based on Islamic misogyny and backwardness, and Middle Eastern women will have no cause to regret its passing.

The twenty-first century must be the century that rids itself of political Islam. . . . Why should Islam be eliminated from the operations of the state instead of modernized and reformed? If someone says that slavery, fascism, or patriarchy can become humane and modernized, I would ask them why they should not be abandoned altogether. In the view of advocates of Islamic reform, if Islam allowed a woman to go to school in a knee-length skirt or to become a judge as long as she does not speak of her sexuality, then it would be acceptable. This is not the improvement that we deserve. Attempts to modernize or reform Islam will only prolong the age-old oppression and subordination of women. Rather than modernize Islam, it must be caged, just as humanity caged Christianity two centuries ago. Islam must become subordinate to secularism and the secular state.

> **EVALUATING THE AUTHORS' ARGUMENTS:**
>
> In this viewpoint, author Azam Kamguian argues that Muslim women throughout the Middle East are denied the right to own property, earn income, and inherit wealth. In the following viewpoint, authors Mary Ali and Anjum Ali contend that Islam grants women the right to own property, earn income, and inherit wealth. How might you explain the discrepancy between the authors' ideas of women under Islam?

Islam Does Not Oppress Women

Mary Ali and Anjum Ali

"The Qur'an and the Traditions of the Prophet . . . are the sources from which every Muslim woman derives her rights."

Mary Ali and Anjum Ali are affiliated with the Institute of Islamic Information and Education, an organization that seeks to elevate the image of Islam and Muslims in North America by providing information about Islamic beliefs and history. In the following viewpoint, they claim that women are afforded many rights under Islam. Ali and Ali claim that under Islam, women are guaranteed civil, political, social, economic, and domestic rights and that women are equal in society with men. Some of the rights Muslim women enjoy are freedom of speech, the right to earn money, and the right to own property, rights which the authors argue many Western women do not enjoy today. The authors believe that the laws of Islam liberate women and ensure they are treated as equals.

AS YOU READ, CONSIDER THE FOLLOWING QUESTIONS:
1. According to the authors, why is it impossible for women to be viewed as evil in Islam?
2. What do the authors say a woman needs to be a skillful parent?
3. According to Ali and Ali, when did the women's liberation movement begin?

oday people think that women are liberated in the West and that the women's liberation movement began in the 20th century. Actually, the women's liberation movement was not begun by women but was revealed by God to a man in the seventh century by the name of Muhammad (Peace be upon him), who is known as the last Prophet of Islam. The Qur'an and the Traditions of the Prophet (*Hadith* or *Sunnah*) are the sources from which every Muslim woman derives her rights and duties.

Human Rights

Islam, fourteen centuries ago, made women equally accountable to God in glorifying and worshipping Him—setting no limits on her moral progress. Also, Islam established a woman's equality in her humanity with men. In the Qur'an, in the first verse of the chapter entitled "Women", God says,

> O mankind! Be careful of your duty toward your Lord who created you from a single soul and from it its mate and from them both have spread abroad a multitude of men and women. Be

A Muslim woman in Malaysia surfs the Internet. Supporters of Islam argue that the religion does not inherently suppress women's rights.

careful of your duty toward Allah in Whom you claim (your rights) of one another, and towards the wombs (that bore you). Lo! Allah has been a Watcher over you. (4:1)

Since men and women both came from the same essence, they are equal in their humanity. Women cannot be by nature evil (as some religions believe) or then men would be evil also. Similarly, neither gender can be superior because it would be a contradiction to equality.

Civil Rights

In Islam, a woman has the basic freedoms of choice and expression based on recognition of her individual personality. First, she is free to choose her religion. The Qur'an states:

There is no compulsion in religion. Right has been made distinct from error. (2:256)

Women are encouraged in Islam to contribute their opinions and ideas. There are many traditions of the Prophet which indicate women would pose questions directly to him and offer their opinions concerning religion, economics and social matters.

A Muslim woman chooses her husband and keeps her name after marriage. A Muslim woman's testimony is valid in legal disputes. In fact, where women are more familiar, their evidence is conclusive.

Social Rights

The Prophet said, "seeking knowledge is a mandate for every Muslim (male and female)". This includes knowledge of the Qur'an and the Hadith as well as other knowledge. Men and women both have the capacity for learning and understanding. Since it is also their obligation to promote good behavior and condemn bad behavior in all spheres of life, Muslim women must acquire the appropriate education to perform this duty in accordance with their own natural talents and interests.

While bearing, raising and teaching of children, providing support to her husband, and maintenance of a home are among the first and very highly regarded roles for a woman, if she has the skills to work outside the home for the good of the community, she may do so as long as her family obligations are met.

Muslim women prepare to vote in a local election in the Philippines. Verse 60:12 of the Qur'an extends the right to vote to women.

Islam recognizes and fosters the natural differences between men and women despite their equality. Some types of work are more suitable for men and other types for women. This in no way diminishes either's efforts or benefits. God will reward both sexes equally for the value of their work, though it may not necessarily be the same activity.

Concerning motherhood, the Prophet said, "Heaven lies under the feet of mothers". This implies that the success of a society can be traced to the mothers who raised it. The first and greatest influence on a person comes from the sense of security, affection, and training received from the mother. Therefore, a woman having children must be educated and conscientious in order to be a skillful parent.

Political Rights

A right given to Muslim women by God 1400 years ago is the right to vote. On any public matter, a woman may voice her opinion and participate in politics. One example, as narrated in the Qur'an (60:12), Muhammad is told that when the believing women come to him and swear their allegiance to Islam, he must accept their oath. This established the right of women to select their leader and publicly declare so. Finally, Islam does not forbid a woman from holding important positions in government. Abdurrahman Ibn Affan consulted many women before he recommended Uthman Ibn Affan to be the Caliph. . . .

Economic Rights

Muslim women have the privilege to earn money, the right to own property, to enter into legal contracts and to manage all of her assets

The Qur'an guarantees the rights of Muslim wives, which include the right to food, shelter, clothing, and kind treatment.

in any way she pleases. She can run her own business and no one has any claim on her earnings, including her husband.

The Qur'an states:

> And in no wise covet those things in which Allah hath bestowed His gifts more freely on some of you than on others; to men is allotted what they earn, and to women, what they earn; but ask Allah of His bounty for Allah hath full knowledge of all things. (4:32)

A woman inherits from her relatives. The Qur'an states:

> For men there is a share in what parents and relatives leave, and for women there is a share of what parents and relatives leave, whether it be little or much—an ordained share. (4:7)

Rights of a Wife

To foster the love and security that comes with marriage, Muslim wives have various rights. The first of the wife's rights is to receive *mahr,* a gift from the husband, which is part of the marriage contract and required for the legality of the marriage.

The second right of a wife is maintenance. Despite any wealth she may have, her husband is obligated to provide her with food, shelter and clothing. He is not forced, however, to spend beyond his capability and his wife is not entitled to make unreasonable demands. The Qur'an states

> Let the man of means spend according to his means, and the man whose resources are restricted, let him spend according to what Allah has given him. Allah puts no burden on any person beyond what He has given him. (65:7)

God tells us men are guardians over women and are afforded the leadership in the family. His responsibility for obeying God extends to guiding his family to obey God at all times.

A wife's rights also extend beyond material needs. She has the right to kind treatment. The Prophet said,

> The most perfect believers are the best in conduct. And the best of you are those who are the best to their wives.

God tells us He created mates and put love, mercy and tranquility between them.

Both men and women have a need for companionship and sexual needs and marriage is designed to fulfill those needs. For one spouse to deny this satisfaction to the other, the temptation exists to seek it elsewhere. . . .

Islam Provides for Women
The Qur'an states:

> And it becomes not a believing man or a believing woman, when Allah and His Messenger, Muhammad (S) have decided on an affair (for them), that they should (after that) claim any say in their affair; and whoso is rebellious to Allah and His Messenger, he verily goes astray in error manifest. (33:36)

The Muslim woman was given a role, duties and rights 1400 years ago that most women do not enjoy today, even in the West. These are from God and are designed to keep balance in society; what may seem unjust or missing in one place is compensated for or explained in another place. Islam is a complete way of life.

EVALUATING THE AUTHORS' ARGUMENTS:

In this viewpoint, the authors contend that Islam is a complete way of life, meaning that its laws are intended to guide all aspects of Muslim society, including the social, economic, and political. In the previous viewpoint, the author argues that Islam must not be used to determine social, economic, and political issues. In your opinion, should a religion be used as the basis for a political system? Why or why not?

The Veil Symbolizes Oppression

Cheryl Benard

> *"Throughout the Islamic world the hijab is often something girls and women wear because they're forced to."*

In the following viewpoint, author Cheryl Benard argues that Muslim women are oppressed by the veil, a type of covering that is traditionally worn by religious women. She contends that the veil is un-Islamic and that the Koran, the Islamic holy book, never ordered women to wear any such covering. Instead, it is the patriarchal societies of the Middle East that have forced women to cover themselves in order to oppress and control them. She describes how women have been assaulted and killed for not wearing the veil. In order for women to be liberated, Benard says they must re-examine their religious texts and interpret them in a way that does not oppress women.

Cheryl Benard is the author of *The Government of God: Iran's Islamic Republic.* She is a senior political scientist at the Rand Corporation, an independent research organization.

AS YOU READ, CONSIDER THE FOLLOWING QUESTIONS:
  1. What happened in Saudi Arabia in March 2002?
  2. Why did Afghan king Amanullah call together an assembly of religious leaders in the 1920s?
  3. What does the author mean when she criticizes Muslim societies for placing the obligation to guarantee public morality "on women alone"?

French President Jacques Chirac has been sharply criticized by Muslim clerics around the world for his recent call for a ban on the Islamic head scarf, or hijab, in French public schools. Mr. Chirac's move has been attacked as a curtailment of personal freedom and an assault on Islam.

But the proposed ban has also kicked loose a debate among Muslims everywhere. Indeed, a growing number of Muslims worldwide are coming forward to say the hijab is not a valid symbol either of freedom or Islam.

A Symbol of Restriction and Intimidation

"Neither the Koran, nor the hadith [the sayings of the prophet Muhammad] require women to wear a head scarf," says Gammal Banna, the Egyptian author of several works on the rights of Muslim women and brother of the founder of the Muslim Brotherhood, the influential radical Islamic movement with offshoots worldwide. While telling *Agence France-Presse* that he did not support the French president's interference in the personal choice to wear a head scarf, Mr. Banna noted, "The head scarf is not an obligation, but derives from an erroneous reading of the Koran."

Nor is the hijab a good symbol for freedom. Throughout the Islamic world the hijab is often something girls and women wear because they're forced to—a symbol of restriction and intimidation, not freedom. Millions of women worldwide are daily threatened—and substantial numbers even assaulted, maimed, or killed—for refusing to wear whatever the local male authorities decide they should be wearing.

In countries such as Saudi Arabia, special religious patrols beat, insult, and arrest women who aren't covered according to their stringent specifications. In Pakistan, Kashmir, and Afghanistan, hundreds of women have been blinded or maimed when acid was thrown on their unveiled faces by male fanatics who considered them improperly dressed. In post-Taliban Afghanistan, women have been raped for daring to think they could now go without the burqa [full-body veil].

In March 2002, 15 Saudi girls ran for their lives when their school caught fire, without wasting precious time to first wrap themselves in their abayas (black robes that are mandatory female attire). Better dead than bare-headed, the religious police decided, and forced the girls back into the burning building and fiery deaths.

This Afghan woman wears a burqa, a veil that completely covers the face.

Oppressive Attire

For most Muslim women, a head scarf is just a small part of oppressive attire that includes large, bulky garments that impair vision, impede movement, stifle breathing, and are unbearably hot in the summer. This, too, is un-Islamic. "God desires ease for you; he does not desire hardship for you," the Koran states.

As a "symbol," the hijab says that women's bodies are sinful, that women really shouldn't be out in public, that there can be no innocent interaction between women and men, and that the obligation for guaranteeing public morality rests on women alone.

Increasingly, Muslim women and their supporters—even in arch-conservative Saudi Arabia, where some of the most severe restrictions on women have the force of law—argue that extreme dress codes for women are not just un-Islamic, but anti-Islamic. The Koran supports their position. "There is no compulsion in religion," it states. A woman who wears the hijab out of fear acquires no merit, and the person exercising the compulsion is committing a sin.

The Koran Does Not Mandate Veiling

When the reformist Afghan King Amanullah decided to liberate his country's women from their stifling burqas in the 1920s, he called

Handelsman. © 2003 by *Newsday.* Reproduced by permission of Tribune Media Services, Inc.

Critics of extensive veils such as the one worn by an Indian woman argue that the Koran only stipulates that Muslim women dress modestly.

together an assembly of the country's most conservative religious leaders, handed them a Koran, and asked them to point to the passage requiring women to veil. The religious leaders couldn't do it, because no such passage exists.

There are three sections in the Koran that deal with the issue of dress. The first instructs men and women to dress modestly. All people are to cover "that which is customarily concealed," in other words, what we think of as "private parts."

A second passage advises the prophet Muhammad to "enjoin the believing women to draw their covering over their bosom. That is more proper, so that they will be respected and not molested."

A third passage deals only with Muhammad's wives. Muhammad didn't like his younger wives to be chatted up by young men who didn't recognize them as members of his household. When fundamentalists argue that Muslim women should conceal themselves, remain secluded, and not interact freely with men, they refer to this passage, which was never intended to apply to average Muslim women: "Wives of the

Prophet, you are not like other women. If you fear Allah, do not be careless in your speech, lest the lecherous should lust after you. Show discretion in what you say. Stay in your homes and do not display your beauty."

Fundamentalists contend that unveiled women inspire lewd thoughts in men, leading them into sin. Islam, however, holds that no one is responsible for the sins of another. The Koran even tells Muslims how to deal with temptation: "Tell the believing men to lower their gaze, and tell the believing women to lower their gaze."

Muslims Should Reexamine Islam

Muhammad was no proponent of sexual segregation. He enjoyed the company of women, sought their advice, nominated them to significant posts in the community such as market supervisor and mosque custodian, and named several of them as authoritative experts to be consulted after his death on the interpretation of Islam. Men and women prayed together in his mosque and attended "co-ed" entertainment there. The prudish apartheid of today's fundamentalists cannot be laid at his feet.

Ironically, France's new secular dress code may end up taking Islamic society a step forward by sending Muslims back to their own religious texts for review. They'll then discover that Islamic orthodoxy never truly required the restrictions on women that conservatives and fundamentalists demand.

EVALUATING THE AUTHORS' ARGUMENTS:

In this viewpoint, the author supports the decision of the French government to ban the wearing of veils in public schools because she believes the veil is a symbol of female oppression. In the following viewpoint, the author criticizes the decision to ban the veil as a violation of women's religious rights. In your opinion, should people have the right to wear religious clothing in public places? How should the issue of religious dress be handled in secular societies, which typically separate religion from public life? Explain your answer.

The Veil Symbolizes Virtue

Sharon Smith

"Islamic dress allows a woman to be looked upon as a human being and not an object."

Sharon Smith is the author of *Women and Socialism: Essays on Women's Liberation* and is a columnist for the newspaper *Socialist Worker.* In the following viewpoint, she argues that Muslim women choose to wear a veil out of a sense of modesty and self-respect. Westerners argue that the veil is a symbol of female oppression. Smith counters that instead, it allows all women to be viewed as a human being first, rather than as an object. Moreover, she argues that Western nations exploit women by encouraging them to bare their bodies, which devalues and objectifies them. She concludes that barring women from wearing the veil is anti-Islam and does not make gains toward their liberation.

AS YOU READ, CONSIDER THE FOLLOWING QUESTIONS:
1. What does the author believe should be a basic human right for women?
2. According to Smith, in what ways has Western society failed to liberate women?
3. Why does the author view the decision to ban the veil in French schools as hypocritical and racist?

Sharon Smith, "Women and Islam," *International Socialist Review,* May/June 2004, pp. 49–59. Copyright © 2004 by *International Socialist Review.* Reproduced by permission.

French Muslim women, such as this student, have protested their government's decision to ban religious paraphernalia, including headscarves, in public schools.

On March 3, [2004,] the French Senate passed a law banning female students from wearing the hijab, the head covering worn by many Muslim women and girls, in public schools starting in September 2004. The new French law prohibits not just the hijab, but all "signs and dress that ostensibly denote the religious belonging of students." It also bans beards and bandanas that denote Islamic affiliation, the Jewish yarmulka, or skullcap, and "conspicuous" Christian crosses. Nevertheless, few in France, where the press has dubbed the ban "the law against the veil," believe the target is anything but the hijab. . . .

French progressives and feminists who support the law view it as a step forward for Muslim women's rights. On December 5, 2003, for example, sixty prominent French women, inluding actors Isabelle Adjani and Emmanuelle Béart, published a petition calling for an outright ban on the hijab, as a "visible symbol of the submission of women." . . .

Banning the Veil Is Racist Hypocrisy

There is something profoundly hypocritical in banning Islamic religious symbols in the name of secularism and gender equality while the French government continues to subsidize private education for the globally influential—and reactionary—Catholic Church, as well as Jewish religious institutions. Beneath French officials' talk of "laïcité" (separation of church and state), the status quo in French society is Christianity. Prime Minister Jean-Pierre Raffarin even described France as "the old land of Christianity" during the debate. The justice minister of one German state justified banning the hijab by stating that German children "have to learn the roots of Christian religion and European culture."

It is just a short leap from the (stated and unstated) assumption of Christian religious and European cultural superiority to outright hostility to Islam. One German state designated the hijab "a symbol of fundamentalism and extremism." Former French Prime Minister Alain Juppé argued, "It's not paranoid to say we're faced with a rise of political and religious fanaticism." Jacques Peyrat, the mayor of Nice—a far-right stronghold—argued in a speech, "Mosques cannot be conceived of as existing within a secular Republic."

Chirac's hostility toward Muslims, France's largest minority, was apparent when he argued on December 6, 2003, "Wearing a veil, whether we want it or not, is a sort of aggression that is difficult for us to accept." Bernard Stasi, head of Chirac's commission, was even more forthright in defending the ban: "We must be lucid—there are in France some behaviors which cannot be tolerated. There are without any doubt forces in France which are seeking to destabilize the republic, and it is time for the republic to act." . . .

Attacks on Islam

In an equally racist manner, the French government has also marketed the hijab ban as a strike against anti-Semitism—despite the fact that hate crimes against French Jews have historically been inflicted by forces of the far right. During the hijab debate, Education Minister Luc Ferry argued that the Middle East conflict "has entered our schools" and that France is facing an anti-Semitism "which is no longer of the extreme right, but of Islamic origin." In November—just weeks before proposing the hijab ban—Chirac announced a new government commission to fight anti-Semitism, which will target the residents of North African neighborhoods for education against anti-Semitism.

In reality, Muslims have been the primary targets of hate crimes in France (and throughout Europe) since the 1960s. Yet France's ministry of the interior does not even include a category for attacks directed against Muslims or North Africans, as it does with anti-Semitic attacks. Norman Madarasz summarized the targeted communities as follows: "In England, with Pakistanis, in Germany, with the Turkish, and in France, Italy, Spain and Portugal, with immigrants from the al-Maghreb North African region: Moroccans, Algerians, Tunisians, Berbers, Cabyls, as well as Palestinians and sub-Saharan Muslims, especially from Mali." . . .

In this context, France's ban on Islamic headscarves can only further inflame anti-Muslim racism. No law reeking of such racist hypocrisy is intended to advance the cause of women's equality. . . .

FAST FACT

The Koran advocates modest dress for Islamic women: "O prophet, tell your wives, your daughters, and the wives of the believers that they shall lengthen their garments. Thus, they will be recognized (as righteous women) and avoid being insulted." (Koran 33:59).

"We Chose the Headscarf"

In the context of imperialism—and the racism that justifies imperialist domination—it is wrong to view the hijab, or other aspects of Islamic culture, only as symbols of women's oppression. Today, the hijab is worn voluntarily by millions of Muslim women around the world as a symbol of cultural pride, often in overt opposition to Western imperialism. After Chirac announced the ban on headscarves, tens of thousands of women wearing the hijab marched in protest across France, chanting slogans such as, "Not our fathers nor our husbands, we chose the headscarf." In London, thousands of young women wearing hijabs also marched, chanting against "racist laws." Their voices should not be ignored.

There is no contradiction between supporting Muslim women protesting the ban on headscarves in France and championing Afghan women in their fight against laws mandating the burqa. Women should have the right to dress as they choose wherever they live, without government interference. This should be a basic human right.

The West Has Not Liberated Women

Moreover, feminists who allowed the Bush administration to equate the lifting of the Islamic veil with liberation,

Many Muslim women throughout the world voluntarily veil themselves because they see the headscarf as a symbol of cultural pride.

Muslim women, such as these demonstrating in Pakistan, prefer the coverage of the veil to the skimpy outfits that are fashionable in the West.

and those who now argue that the France's hijab ban is a step toward women's equality, perform a disservice to the fight for genuine women's liberation, East and West. Journalist Natasha Walter recently expressed the common view among Western feminists: "Many women in the west find the headscarf deeply problematic. One of the reasons we find it so hateful is because the whole trajectory of feminism in the west has been tied up with the freedom to uncover ourselves."

But the "freedom to uncover" can bring women no closer to genuine equality in a sexist society. In societies the world over, "uncovering" merely leads to greater sexual objectification. In the U.S., eating disorders have reached epidemic proportions among young women, cosmetic surgery is one of the fastest-growing branches of modern medicine, and Hooters is a national restaurant chain. Jiggle movies like "Charlie's Angels" and "Tomb Raider" offer some of the best opportunities for career advancement for female actresses in Hollywood. And cartoon shows such as "Stripperella"—starring Erotica Jones, "a stripper by night and a superhero by later night"—target an ever-younger audience. Soon to join the primetime lineup is "Hef's Superbunnies," a cartoon about Playboy Playmates who fight evil.

Turkish society illustrates why "secularism" and "Westernization" do not automatically lead to women's liberation. Although Turkey's population is overwhelmingly Muslim, its government bans the hijab for women in educational institutions and government offices. But Turkey has imported Western sexist culture as well, including an endless barrage of demeaning sexist imagery. As political economist Behzad Yaghmaian described on a recent visit to Turkey, "Pictures of half-naked women were exhibited on billboards and in daily newspapers."

A Human Being, Not an Object

Yaghmaian described a woman student from Istanbul University, who said, "Hijab sends an important message that a person does not have to see my body to have a conversation with me." This sentiment is valid and should not be dismissed by feminists. As a young Egyptian woman told reporters some years ago, she prefers the hijab because, "Many men treat women as objects, look at their beauty; the Islamic dress allows a woman to be looked upon as a human being and not an object."

> **EVALUATING THE AUTHORS' ARGUMENTS:**
>
> In the viewpoint you just read, the author argues that the veil is worn with pride and virtue. In the previous viewpoint, the author describes the veil as an instrument of oppression. After reading both viewpoints, how do you view the veil? Explain your reasoning.

Chapter 3

What Does the Future Hold for Islam?

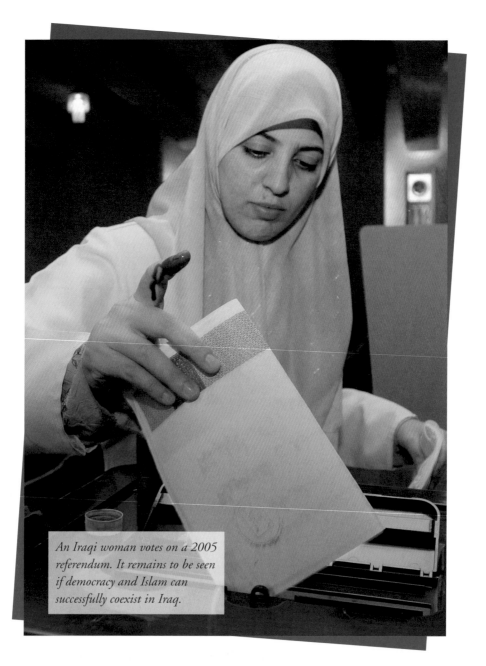

An Iraqi woman votes on a 2005 referendum. It remains to be seen if democracy and Islam can successfully coexist in Iraq.

Muslims Must Oppose Radical Islam

Jeff Jacoby

"'We cannot clear our names unless we own up to the shameful fact that terrorism has become an Islamic enterprise.'"

In the following viewpoint, author Jeff Jacoby complains that Muslims are often silent on the issue of terrorism committed in the name of Islam. He cites the Beslan school shootings of 2004, in which Muslim terrorists killed students, teachers, and parents. Criticism of the terrorists' actions, in the author's opinion, was muted and insincere: The leaders of Muslim nations who condemned the terror are known to be sponsors of terror themselves, while other Islamic organizations ignored the fact that the terrorists were Muslim. The author calls on the world's Muslims to speak out against radical Islam in order to prove that they truly condemn terrorism committed in the name of their faith.

Jeff Jacoby is a columnist for the *Boston Globe,* from which this viewpoint was taken.

AS YOU READ, CONSIDER THE FOLLOWING QUESTIONS:
1. Why does the author consider Sheik Muhammad Sayyid Tantawi's denunciation of terrorism to be meaningless?
2. What did Prince Abdullah of Saudi Arabia tell Russian president Vladimir Putin?
3. What were the thoughts of Islamic cleric Omar Bakri Mohammed regarding the Beslan murders?

Jeff Jacoby, "Where Is the Muslim Outrage?" *The Boston Globe,* September 9, 2004. Copyright © 2004 by Globe Newspaper Company. Reproduced by permission.

They are still burying the victims of the latest atrocity committed, some believe, in the name of Islam—the slaughter of
hundreds of children, teachers, and parents in an elementary
school in Beslan, Russia [in September 2004]. And from Muslims the
world over, as usual, has come mostly silence.

Muslims Are Too Quiet on the Issue of Terrorism

There have been no public demonstrations by Muslims anxious to
make it clear how outraged they are that anyone could commit such
unspeakable deeds for their version of Islam. There has been no
anguished outcry by Islam's leading imams and sheiks. Prominent
Muslim organizations in the West have not called press conferences

Russian women grieve at the site of the Beslan school siege, while a school boy observes a moment of silence. The horrific attack was perpetrated by Muslim militants.

THE MUSLIM WORLD'S REACTION TO THE HUMILIATION OF PRISONERS AT ABU GHRAIB...

...AND TO THE MASSACRE OF SCHOOL CHILDREN IN RUSSIA.

Ariail. © 2004 by *The State*/Distributed by Newspaper Enterprise Association, Inc. Reproduced by permission.

to express their disgust. Once again the world has witnessed a savage episode of Islamist terror, and once again it strains to hear a convincing rejection of the terrorists from those who should care most about Islam's reputation.

That is not to say there has been no criticism at all. Crown Prince Abdullah of Saudi Arabia telephoned Russian President Vladimir Putin to assure him that "this terrorist act . . . goes against religious teachings and violates human and moral values." Syria's official news agency decried the massacre as "a terrorist, cowardly action." Sheik Muhammad Sayyid Tantawi of Al-Azhar University in Cairo lambasted the murderers for "taking Islam as cover" and said that "those who carry out the kidnappings are criminals, not Muslims."

But these are boilerplate denunciations, practically meaningless—particularly when they come from sources that sustain Islamist fanaticism (Saudi Arabia), shelter and support terrorists (Syria), or defend suicide bombers as praiseworthy "martyrs" (Tantawi). They condemn no terrorists or terror organizations by name. They offer no help in destroying the infrastructure that recruits, funds, and trains them. And they contain no hint that the global scourge of Islamofascist jihad is a cancer eating away at the Muslim world.

A group of Italian Muslims demonstrate their rejection of Islamic terrorists by carrying signs that read: "No to Violence," "Yes to Dialogue," and "No to Terrorism."

Ignoring the Facts

The Council on American-Islamic Relations [CAIR], which issues dozens of press releases every month, had nothing to say about the bloodbath in Russia until I requested a comment. The statement CAIR then issued doesn't even acknowledge that the killers were Muslim:

"No words can describe the horror and grief generated by the deaths of so many innocent people at the hands of those who dishonor the cause they espouse. We offer sincere condolences to the families of the victims and call for a swift resolution to the conflict in that troubled region." At least CAIR went through the motions of condemning the butchery. Other voices preached a different message altogether.

Ali Abdullah, an Islamic scholar in Bahrain, announced that the bloodshed in Beslan "is the work of the Israelis who want to tarnish the image of Muslims." In London, Islamist cleric Omar Bakri Mohammed told the *Daily Telegraph* : "If an Iraqi Muslim carried out an attack like that in Britain, it would be justified because Britain has carried out acts of terrorism in Iraq."

The Courage to Condemn

Fortunately, a few Muslim commentators have denounced the evil being done in the name of Islam, and have done so courageously and unambiguously. (The Middle East Media Research Institute has compiled their reactions at www.memri.org.) One in particular stands out: an extraordinary column in the pan-Arabic daily *Al-Sharq Al-Awsat* by Abdel Rahman al-Rashed, the manager of the Al-Arabiya news channel.

"It is a certain fact that not all Muslims are terrorists," he begins, "but it is equally certain, and exceptionally painful, that almost all terrorists are Muslims."

> The hostage-takers of the children in Beslan were Muslims. The hostage-takers and murderers of the Nepalese chefs and workers in Iraq were also Muslims. . . . The majority of those who manned the suicide bombings against buses, vehicles, schools, houses, and buildings all over the world were Muslim. . . . Does all this tell us anything about ourselves, our societies, and our culture? . . .

> We cannot tolerate in our midst those who abduct journalists, murder civilians, explode buses; we cannot accept them as related to us. . . . They are the people who have smeared Islam and stained its image. We cannot clear our names unless we own up to the shameful fact that terrorism has become an Islamic enterprise; an almost exclusive monopoly implemented by Muslim men and women.

When it is no longer astonishing to encounter such sentiments in the Muslim world, we will know that the corner has been turned in the war against Islamist terror.

EVALUATING THE AUTHOR'S ARGUMENTS:

In this viewpoint, author Jeff Jacoby says that the war on terror will have made clear progress when sentiments like those of columnist Abdel Rahman al-Rashed are no longer out of the ordinary. What do you think he means by this statement? In your opinion, what sets al-Rashed's work apart from the other condemnations of terrorism that Jacoby mentions?

Muslims Must Reject Western Values

Yusuf al-Khabbaz

"Sadly, young Muslims today know everything about singers and actors, but they ignore or lack knowledge about the Palestinian struggle or the ongoing colonization of Iraq."

In the following viewpoint Yusuf al-Khabbaz urges Muslims around the world to reject the values of the West and embrace Islamic culture. He argues that the West has pushed its systems of language, education, and entertainment upon Muslim peoples, forcing them to lose touch with their own values and culture. As a result, al-Khabbaz says, the Muslim mind has become colonized, meaning that Muslims have been wrongfully turned into cultural subjects of the West. He laments that Muslims have been taught to see themselves as backward and barbaric. Finaly, al-Khabbaz concludes that it is Western peoples who have perpetrated bloody wars and forcefully imposed their culture on other peoples.

Yusuf al-Khabbaz is the pen name of a Middle Eastern academic who writes about Islamic affairs. He is a regular contributor to *Crescent International,* a newsmagazine of the global Islamist movement.

AS YOU READ, CONSIDER THE FOLLOWING QUESTIONS:
1. Why does al-Khabbaz believe it is important for Muslims to learn languages other than English?
2. What is the "mental environment," and why does the author consider it a form of mental colonization?
3. According to the author, how do the governments of Muslim countries cater to the whims of Americans?

C olonialism is now usually understood as a period of history when the European and American powers forcibly and physically held and exploited territories throughout what is now called the "Third World," from which they drew fabulous wealth. . . .

In the 20th century two massively destructive "world wars" virtually levelled Europe and Japan, and weakened the colonial powers (except America, which was strengthened and able to maintain its colonial status for a while longer). After 1945 a wave of "independence" movements emerged, independence generally being taken to mean the time when the colonial powers physically left. However, the systems the colonizers put in place—for health, education, science, technology, law, etc.—ensured that the formerly colonized, supposedly newly independent peoples would not do anything very different from what the colonizers had intended in the first place, so that the "third world" would remain subordinate to the Western world. This ongoing condition of continuing the policies and ways of life that were initially forced upon the "third world" under direct colonization is what is usually called "mental colonization." . . .

Decolonizing the Muslim Mind

Western education is a key factor in maintaining colonized minds, even to the point that it may be difficult or impossible for people to imagine surviving without a formal Western education. The crucial question to ask is, "What is the goal of education?" Answering that question leads to bigger questions, such as, "What kind of person do I want to be?" Some people want to be American, or French, or British, so they choose a form of schooling for that goal. While it may serve

Catrow. © 2001 by Copley News Service. Reproduced by permission.

them well personally, such a goal is not necessarily in the best interests of anyone else. Beyond that, it is certainly a stubborn illusion of colonialism that the type of schooling one gets in the West is somehow better than what is available elsewhere. . . .

Reject the Hedonistic Culture of the West

The mass media, which include entertainment and advertising, are part of what has been called the "mental environment," and to the extent that this mental environment is being controlled and shaped by a few forces that basically think the same way, at the expense of other ways, it is colonization. Most of the "independent" governments ruling the former "third world" today, including the Muslim world, are participating in the media-perpetrated colonization of the minds of their youth. They allow entertainments from the West to flood the mental environment by means of television and the print media. These governments do not have the power to prevent the hedonistic culture that is being promoted throughout the world, including many Muslim communities in North Africa, the Middle East, Pakistan, Malaysia and elsewhere. Sadly, young Muslims today know everything about singers and actors, but they ignore or lack knowledge about the Palestinian struggle or the ongoing colonization of Iraq. But looking toward governments to solve this problem is part of the problem: almost all governments today are part of the colonial system, either as good subjects or bad subjects. The hope lies, then, with the non-subjects, those people who are thinking and acting beyond the sway of colonialism, modernism, globalism and all the systems invading non-Western societies today. . . .

Hundreds of young men line up for the grand opening of a McDonald's in Egypt. The American chain has opened several locations in the Middle East, stirring huge controversy.

Our Minds Are Under Occupation

Language also plays a role in mental colonialism, although it is more difficult to deal with. English is the language most often associated with colonialism today, and it is fast becoming a global language, often at the expense of local languages. All languages encode reality in a particular way, by using metaphorical and rhetorical structures to represent physical objects and life experiences. English is no different. To become thoroughly decolonized, then, one has to learn, or relearn, another language. . . .

This is sadly apparent today, for example, as when the governments of states in which Muslims now live continue to fall over themselves to cater to the whims of the Americans, revising school curricula and promoting foolish entertainment, most often at the expense of local languages and cultures.

Mecca-Cola was introduced by a Saudi company in order to boycott the spread of American products in the Middle East.

In a manner of speaking, then, our minds are under occupation, in much the same way as our lands are under occupation. This problem deserves constant vigilance, and needs to be thought about and acted upon daily. . . .

Muslims Should Embrace Their Own Culture

One reason why many peoples of the "third world," Muslims included, cannot think in the way necessary to decolonize their minds, is that they no longer follow or even respect their own traditions. Part of this is the result of colonization: we have lost confidence; we have become uncertain of ourselves, even ashamed of who we are, because of the constant chorus telling us that we are backward, repressive, violent, and a host of other accusations. But who is making these accusations? No people in the history of humanity has been more backward, repressive and violent than those who are telling us what to do today, the proponents of Western "civilization." How many people did they kill in their world wars [in the twentieth] century? 100 million? 150 million? Perhaps they ought to look more carefully at themselves before they accuse Muslims of anything; regardless of whether they do so or not, we must.

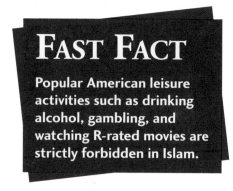

FAST FACT

Popular American leisure activities such as drinking alcohol, gambling, and watching R-rated movies are strictly forbidden in Islam.

Islam, as most Muslims know, is a way of life, an ethical code and a body of law, not "just a religion"; within it are many features that can become part of living a decolonized lifestyle. . . .

Muslims Remain Colonized

Decolonizing the mind will not be an overnight success, but there are some things anyone can do straightaway, once the true nature of the problem is understood. So let me state the problem as succinctly as I can: we are, all or most of us, thinking and acting in ways that are destructive and often not even logical, but which continue to benefit a small global elite. In order to force us to remain colonized, we have been alienated from our humanity, our environment, our traditions and our religions, in the name of progress, civilization, globalization and a host of other euphemisms for colonialism. . . .

Muslims and the followers of other religions are increasingly wondering whether "the end is near"; there are a lot of "end of days" predictions floating around the internet today, from various quarters. But historically people have always thought that their problems were clear portents of the end of the world. The only thing we can be sure of is that only Allah knows when that day will come, or when the Awaited Savior, and any other promised salvation, will arrive. It is surely a sign of our colonized minds that, just because Western "civilization" has been exposed in all its barbarity in Iraq and Palestine, by complicity or direct action, or just because the global economy is faltering, or because Americans are realizing they are living in a miserable police state, we do not realise that all this does not necessarily mean the end of the world for everyone else (or indeed anyone else). In fact, this is perhaps the most opportune moment to look outside the weird West, its spheres of influence, and especially its immense problems, to where alternatives and hope still wait for us to go looking for them.

EVALUATING THE AUTHOR'S ARGUMENTS:

In this viewpoint author Yusuf al-Khabbaz complains that Western culture has been unfairly forced on people in Muslim societies. What is your opinion of this complaint—do you think it is legitimate, or is it unfounded? Should one country be able to export elements of its culture, such as its movies or its standards of fashion, to another? Explain your answer.

Viewpoint 3

Democracy and Islam Are Compatible

Shirin Ebadi

In the following viewpoint Iranian activist Shirin Ebadi argues that Islam is compatible with democracy and human rights, but it has been co-opted by corrupt Muslim leaders and become a tool for exploitation and oppression. These leaders have deviated from the core tenants of Islam, which the author contends include a commitment to democracy and preserving equality among all peoples. For example, the author recounts how the Prophet Muhammad allowed both Muslims and non-Muslims to live freely in the Islamic world, illustrating dedication to freedom of religion, a key tenet of democracy. If Muslims were to reclaim their religion from those who have corrupted it, the author argues, they would realize that Islamic states can be fully committed to preserving democracy, equality, and human rights.

Shirin Ebadi is an Iranian activist for human rights, democracy, women, and children. In October 2004 she became the first Muslim to receive the Nobel Peace Prize for her work.

"We can remain Muslims while embracing the principles of human rights and democracy."

Shirin Ebadi, "Islam, Democracy, and Human Rights: Dr. Shirin Ebadi's Address at Syracuse University, May 10, 2004," *Orangebytes,* vol. 2, May 2004. Reproduced by permission of the author.

AS YOU READ, CONSIDER THE FOLLOWING QUESTIONS:
1. According to the author, what was one outcome of the European Renaissance?
2. Ebadi describes how the Prophet Muhammad believed the elite members of his tribe had no priority over other believers. How does this reflect a democratic ideal?
3. According to the author, what do Muslim intellectuals need to tell the Muslim masses about?

A few centuries ago the European Renaissance lessened [the] perceived incompatibility between democracy and religion, while continually strengthening democracy. Yet in the Eastern world and in Muslim countries in particular, the thorny relationship between religion and democracy is yet to follow the European blueprint. It is nevertheless the case today that the tangled and complicated relationship between state and religion is fueling fiery political disputes in the Middle East and resistance to democracy in the region is, at least in part, due to the contention that Islam is incompatible with human rights.

Obviously, this "Islam" is only what the state defines it to be, i.e., its own ideology, completely discarding the interpretations of other Muslims as to what constitutes Shari'a (or divine law). In reality, what we have ended up with in these countries is "state religion" rather than a "religious state." These guardians of state religion, who arrogate to themselves the exclusive authority to interpret the will or intentions of God, brand whoever opposes them as an infidel or deviant. Using this rather convenient ploy, these demagogic politicians force their political opponents into silence, robbing the populace of their spirit to resist. After all, ordinary people are more willing to fight mortal rulers than to differ with the religion of their ancestors.

FAST FACT

With over 210 million Muslims, Indonesia is the world's largest Islamic country. It is also a democracy.

Islam Has Many Democratic Elements

In contrast to these governments, Islamic reformers and religious intellectuals, regardless of their nationality, are a potential united front. The formation of this multinational coalition, backed by valid jurisprudential interpretations, seeking guidance from the spirit of the holy Quran,

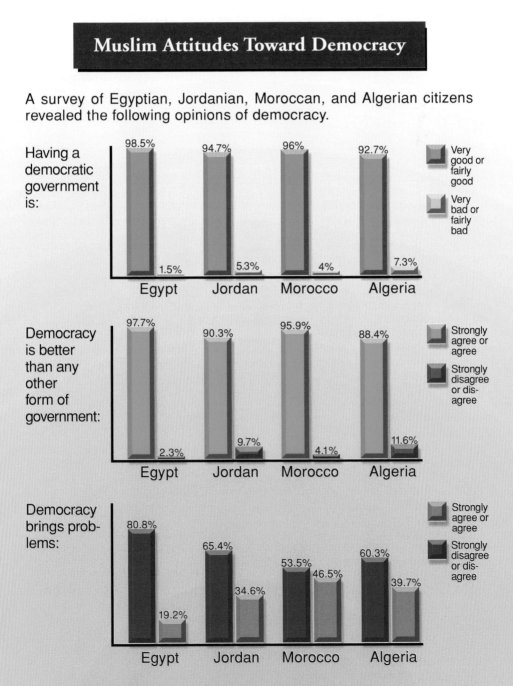

Muslim Attitudes Toward Democracy

A survey of Egyptian, Jordanian, Moroccan, and Algerian citizens revealed the following opinions of democracy.

Having a democratic government is:

	Egypt	Jordan	Morocco	Algeria
Very good or fairly good	98.5%	94.7%	96%	92.7%
Very bad or fairly bad	1.5%	5.3%	4%	7.3%

Democracy is better than any other form of government:

	Egypt	Jordan	Morocco	Algeria
Strongly agree or agree	97.7%	90.3%	95.9%	88.4%
Strongly disagree or disagree	2.3%	9.7%	4.1%	11.6%

Democracy brings problems:

	Egypt	Jordan	Morocco	Algeria
Strongly agree or agree	80.8%	65.4%	53.5%	60.3%
Strongly disagree or disagree	19.2%	34.6%	46.5%	39.7%

Source: World Values Survey, 1995–2001.

and resolving to resist oppressive regimes heralds the emancipation of Muslims. This unified front has no name, no leader, no central head-quarters or branches, and yet it is ingrained in the minds and sensibil-ities of every enlightened Muslim, who while safeguarding their ances-tral faith, also happen to respect democracy, do not tolerate rule by fiat [that is, rule by decree] and refuse to follow the misguided proclama-tions of religious authorities. Islam, in its essence, is a religion of equal-ity. The Prophet Muhammad used to say that the elite of his own tribe have no priority over other believers. After his triumphant return to [the holy city of] Mecca, the Prophet Muhammad established an Islamic

An Iraqi man reviews instructions on how to vote. Many Muslims are hopeful that democracy will take root in Iraq.

Many Muslims point to the democratic society established by the Prophet Muhammad as proof that democracy and Islam can mix.

state and ruled as the political leader and law giver for a number of years. He asked both Muslims and non-Muslims to swear allegiance to the new faith, a practice akin to voting in our present day and age. Some people did not swear allegiance but managed to live freely within the boundaries of the Islamic world.

In reality, then, lack of democratization in the Islamic world does not emanate from the essence of Islam. Rather, it is due to the unwillingness for numerous reasons of Islamic states to embrace an interpretation of Islam that is compatible with human rights, preserves individual and social freedoms, and advocates democratic statecraft. For these reasons, the dominant culture in Muslim societies, including the political culture, is in need of overhaul and reform in order to empower people to understand social realities with open eyes and to write laws that are both compatible with the spirit of Islam and address the needs of our era.

Muslims Must Relearn Islam

The most important step for this cultural evolution is to teach the inclusiveness of Islamic faith. Muslims need to learn about the dynamic spirit of Islam and to recognize that one could be a faithful Muslim and accept modernity at the same time. We need to learn that we can remain Muslims while embracing the principles of human rights and democracy, and more significantly, while implementing them. . . .

Alas, authoritarian regimes manage to hide behind the shield of Islam and continue to oppress their citizens. Muslim intellectuals should try to connect with the Muslim masses, through any means and methods available, and familiarize people with the dynamic spirit of Islam. These intellectuals should subsequently expose the false claims of the despotic rulers in such a way that mass audiences can understand and relate to their words and ideas. We should bear in mind that criticizing the policies of self-proclaimed Islamic states will not be effective and will not resonate with the majority of the public unless the critics can point out how the actions of the ruling elite have deviated from or violated the core foundations of Islam.

EVALUATING THE AUTHORS' ARGUMENTS:

In this viewpoint, Shirin Ebadi argues that the core values of Islam include a commitment to individual rights and democracy, and she believes that democracy can take root in Islamic societies. In the following viewpoint, author Edmund O'Sullivan argues that the core values of Islam include a commitment to the group and to the obedience of sharia law, and believes that democracy cannot take root in Islamic societies. After reading both viewpoints, what place do you believe democracy can have in Islamic societies? Is democracy compatible with Islam? Why or why not?

Democracy and Islam Are Incompatible

Edmund O'Sullivan

"The billions of dollars now being spent to make Iraq a model, Western-style country are being wasted."

In the following viewpoint, Edmund O'Sullivan argues that democracy is not compatible with Islam. He argues that the problem stems from different understandings of the importance of the individual. In Western societies, O'Sullivan explains, individual rights are valued above everything else, and this is a main idea of democracy. In the democratic United States, for example, no one can tell an individual what to wear or buy or eat, provided it is within reason and does not infringe on anyone else's rights. In Islamic societies, however, the interests of the group are more important than those of the individual because society is bound by the rules of the Koran, which are followed by the entire Muslim community. In such societies, the pursuit of individual rights, especially when they conflict with religious rules, is viewed as selfish and shortsighted. Therefore, the author argues that the individualism of democracy is at odds with the group mentality that is valued in Islamic societies, and thus democracy will not take hold in Islamic countries.

Edmund O'Sullivan is the editorial director of the *Middle East Economic Digest,* from which this viewpoint was taken.

AS YOU READ, CONSIDER THE FOLLOWING QUESTIONS:
1. According to O'Sullivan, what events challenged the idea that political Islam was just a fad?
2. Why does the author believe the money being spent to turn Iraq into a democracy might go to waste?
3. What does O'Sullivan mean when he writes that in Islamic societies, "government exists to enforce obligations, not protect rights"?

The vitality of Islam in the Middle East continues to bamboozle Western leaders and intellectuals. But there was a time when the world thought it knew what was likely to happen in the Middle East. Thirty years ago, when I first started seriously to study the Arab and Islamic world, the conventional wisdom was that secularism would triumph there as it had done in the West. Communism and nationalism were then believed to be much more potent than a supposedly declining religious movement.

FAST FACT

Islam is viewed by its followers as a comprehensive guide to all aspects of life. This makes the typical democratic notion that church and state should be separate difficult for some Muslim societies to embrace.

Islamic Movements Have Flourished

There was a shift of thinking after the Iranian government was toppled in a [religious] revolution led by the Ayatollah Khomeini that reached a climax on 11 February 1979. Islam attracted fresh attention but many believed religion was being manipulated by Iranian communists and secular anti-regime forces.

Nevertheless, a new consensus emerged that argued Islam was going through a period of revival but could be driven back into the shadows by force. The end of the 1980–88 Gulf war [between Iraq and

Iran] as an effective draw and the suppression of the [Islamist group] Muslim Brotherhood in Egypt were seen to be evidence of this trend.

The belief that political Islam was a fad was undermined by the emergence of a popular Islamist movement in Algeria in the late 1980s and similar trends throughout the Muslim world.

So, by the end of the 1990s, a third consensus developed which conceded that Islam was the most dynamic political factor in the Middle East and that it was here to stay. Its robust nature has become

The Ayatollah Khomeini (right) established the Islamic Republic of Iran in 1979. Since then Iran has been known for its repression and fundamentalism.

more evident since 11 September 2001. America has declared war against every Islamist movement on earth. None, including the Taleban of Afghanistan, have been comprehensively defeated. The mullahs [Islamic leaders] of Iran have strengthened their grip on power. Elections in Iraq [in 2005] are likely to produce a government with a strong Islamic complexion. Islamic Jihad and Hamas are the most dynamic elements of the Palestinian resistance in the Occupied Territories. This pattern is repeated in every Muslim country practically without exception.

The Reality Is That Muslims Want Islamic Government

The prevailing view is that political Islam can no longer be ignored or repressed. The new Western policy is to win over the people of Islamic countries by encouraging democracy, free expression and free markets. Conventional politicians in the Western image will develop and religious leaders will retire to the mosque.

The third consensus, however, is as wrong as the two it has displaced. It fails to recognise that Islamic thinking is coherent and genuinely appealing in Muslim countries. Western political thought argues

Wolverton. © 2004 by Cagle Cartoons, Inc. Reproduced by permission.

A Muslim woman burns American and Israeli flags to protest the overthrow of Saddam Hussein, the former dictator of Iraq.

that society is made up of individuals motivated by utilitarianism, or the pursuit of happiness. Government is there to correct market failures, provide defence and protect rights. President Bush is so convinced by this approach that he claims it is divinely ordained.

Islamic political theory, in contrast, starts with the group and puts the interests of the community of the faithful above those of the individual. The pursuit of happiness, which often looks like vulgar hedonism, is viewed as illusory. Islam argues that humanity's purpose is to reconcile itself with the wishes of its maker as defined in the Sharia. Government exists to enforce obligations, not protect rights.

This approach has a much longer pedigree than the new-fangled initiatives being developed in Washington and London. And it is far more popular. Every time people in Muslim societies have been given the chance to express an opinion, they have opted for the Islamic over the Western political model. Why? Because it makes at least as much sense and is more relevant to low-income societies that cannot afford the excesses of Western materialism.

The Middle East Will Not Be Democratized

For these reasons, the Western political model will struggle to take root, and not only in the Middle East. The latest attempt to westernise the Islamic world [that is, the war in Iraq] could provoke a reaction that might overwhelm the modest beachheads it has so far established in the region.

If this argument is correct, the billions of dollars now being spent to make Iraq a model, Western-style country, are being wasted. It may even, in the end, produce an even more resolutely anti-Western regime than the one that was replaced in April [2003].

EVALUATING THE AUTHOR'S ARGUMENTS:

Edmund O'Sullivan writes that democracy is less attractive to "low-income societies that cannot afford the excesses of Western materialism." What do you think he means by this statement? What bearing does it have on his discussion about individualism, democracy, and Islam?

Glossary

abaya: A loose, usually black robe worn by Muslim women covering the body from head to toe and often worn with a head scarf and veil. Similar to a burka.

Allah: The Arabic name for God.

burka: A long garment that covers the entire body except for the eyes. Also called a "chador," it is typically worn by some Muslim women. Also spelled *burqa, bourkha, burkha, burga,* or *burqua.*

caliph: Successor or representative; for example, Muhammad was God's representative and the caliphs were Muhammad's representatives.

fiqh: Islamic law and judicial procedure.

five pillars of Islam: The profession of faith (*shahada*), the daily prayers (*salat*), almsgiving (*zakat*), the fast during Ramadan (*sawm*), and the pilgrimage to Mecca (*hajj*).

hadith: The sayings and actions of the prophet Muhammad as remembered and recorded by his companions, later assembled into several multivolume collections. They are used as a guide for law, religious practice, and proper behavior.

hijab: A head scarf worn by Muslim women, sometimes including a veil that covers the face except for the eyes.

Islam: Submission to God.

jihad: A struggle or effort to reform, either as an individual or as the Muslim community; a war under religious auspices.

Koran (Qur'an): The holy book of Islam. Muslims believe the Koran was received by Muhammad from God over a period of twenty-two years, memorized by his companions, and written and compiled into a single text after his death.

madrassa: An Islamic school.

mullah: A title of respect for religious teachers and jurists, especially in Iran; literally, "master."

al Qaeda: An international terrorist organization founded in the 1980s by Osama bin Laden. Al Qaeda is responsible for several attacks against the United States, including September 11, 2001.

Ramadan: The ninth month of the Islamic calendar and the month of fasting.

secularism: Keeping religious ideas from influencing political decisions; the separation of church and state.

September 11 Commission Report: The authoritative report on the events leading up to the terrorist attacks of September 11, 2001. The report was issued on July 22, 2004.

sharia: The body of Islamic law found in or inferred from the Koran, the sunna, and the hadith.

sunna: The customary behavior of Muhammad that is used as a guide to proper behavior; literally, "the well-worn path."

Taliban: The former rulers of Afghanistan. The Taliban were overthrown by the United States in October 2001 for sheltering al Qaeda terrorist Osama bin Laden.

Tawhid: God's oneness or unity.

ulema (ulama): The community of legal scholars in a Muslim community.

ummah: The worldwide community of Muslims.

USA Patriot Act: A set of laws passed shortly after the September 11, 2001, terrorist attacks that expanded the power of authorities to monitor and prosecute alleged terrorists.

Wahhabism: A strict form of Islam practiced in Saudi Arabia.

Facts About Islam

Editor's Note: These facts can be used in reports or papers to reinforce or add credibility when making important points or claims.

Islam was founded in the seventh century A.D. by the prophet Muhammad.

Western numbers, such as 1, 2, 3, 4, 5, are called Arabic numbers because the notation system was taught to Europeans by Islamic Arab mathematicians sometime in the Middle Ages.

The word *Islam* is typically translated as "submission to God." It is derived from the Arabic word *salam,* which means "peace."

Muslims worship God directly. Religious leaders do not have any divine characteristics; people and objects are not considered holy.

The Koran contains a lot of the same stories found in the Hebrew Bible, or Christian Old Testament, as well as additional material.

There are two main sects of Islam: Sunni and Shiite. The majority of the world's Muslims are Sunnis.

Muslims follow the lunar calendar, and thus their holidays shift from year to year on the Christian calendar by approximately eleven days.

There are two major holidays in Islam: *Eid al-Adha* is at the end of the pilgrimage to Mecca and *Eid al-Fitr* is at the end of Ramadan. Ramadan is the ninth month of the lunar calendar, the time when it is thought that the prophet Muhammad received the Koran.

Islam Around the World

Though frequently used together, "Muslim" and "Arab" are not synonymous. A Muslim is a person who follows the religion of Islam. "Arab" is an ethnic identity that refers to a person from the Arabian peninsula.

Most Arabs are Muslim, but most Muslims are not Arabs. While more than 90 percent of Arabs are Muslims, just 25 percent of the world's Muslims are Arabs.

Islam has approximately 1.2 billion followers. That means that one in every five people on the planet is a Muslim.

With over 210 million Muslims, Indonesia is the world's largest Islamic country. The countries with the next largest numbers of Muslims are

Pakistan, Bangladesh, and India. There are even Muslims in China—more than 50 million.

According to the Hartford Institute for Religious Research, the world-wide ethnicity of Muslims is as follows:

- South-Central Asian, 33 percent;
- African American, 30 percent;
- Arab, 25 percent;
- African, 3 percent;
- Southeast Asian, 2 percent;
- European, 2 percent;
- Other, 5 percent.

Islam is the fastest-growing religion in the world.

Islam is the second largest of the three major monotheistic religions, the others being Christianity and Judaism.

Islam in America

Because the U.S. census does not collect religious information from citizens, it is unclear exactly how many Muslims live in the United States. Estimates by various institutions are as follows:

- 1.8 million (Graduate Center of the City University of New York, 2001)
- 1.9–2.8 million (National Opinion Research Center of the University of Chicago, 2000)
- 3 million (Middle East Forum in Philadelphia)
- 4 million (*Annual Yearbook of American and Canadian Churches,* 2000)
- 5 million (Charles Kimball, Wake Forest University Religion Department chairman, 2002)
- 6 million (Council on American-Islamic Relations, 2002)

The first Muslim communities in America were in the Midwest. In North Dakota, Muslims organized for prayers in the very early 1900s; in Indiana, an Islamic center was begun as early as 1914; Cedar Rapids, Iowa, is the home of the oldest mosque still in use.

According to the U.S. Department of State's Bureau of International Information Programs:

- There are 1,209 mosques in the United States
- Two million American Muslims are associated with a mosque

- Since 1994, the number of mosques has increased by 25 percent
- Between 17 and 30 percent of American Muslims are converts
- Nearly 90 percent of U.S. mosques have some Asian, African American, and Arab members
- About 7 percent of U.S. mosques are attended by a single ethnic group

The U.S. Department of State estimates that the ethnicity of American Muslims is as follows:

- South Asian (Pakistani, Indian, Bangladeshi, Afghani), 33 percent;
- African American, 30 percent;
- Arab, 25 percent;
- Sub-Saharan African, 3.4 percent;
- European (Bosnian, Tartar, Kosovar), 2.1 percent;
- White American, 1.6 percent;
- Southeast Asian (Malaysian, Indonesian, Filipino), 1.3 percent;
- Caribbean, 1.2 percent;
- Turkish, 1.1 percent;
- Iranian, 0.7 percent;
- Hispanic/Latino, 0.6 percent.

According to the Council on American-Islamic Relations (CAIR), there were 1,717 reports of harassment, violence, and other discriminatory acts against American Muslims in the first six months following the September 11, 2001, terrorist attacks.

Organizations to Contact

American-Arab Anti-Discrimination Committee (ADC)
4201 Connecticut Ave. NW, Suite 300, Washington, DC 20008
(202) 244-2990
e-mail: ADC@adc.org
Web site: www.adc.org

This organization fights anti-Arab stereotyping in the media and works to protect Arab Americans from discrimination and hate crimes. It publishes a bimonthly newsletter, the *Chronicle;* issue papers and special reports; community studies; legal, media, and educational guides; and action alerts.

AMIDEAST
1730 M St. NW, Suite 1100, Washington, DC 20036-4505
(202) 776-9600
e-mail: inquiries@amideast.org
Web site: www.amideast.org

AMIDEAST promotes understanding and cooperation between Americans and the people of the Middle East and North Africa through education and development programs. It publishes a number of books for all age groups, including *Islam: A Primer.*

Arab World and Islamic Resources and School Services (AWAIR)
2137 Rose St., Berkeley, CA 94709
(510) 704-0517
e-mail: awair@igc.apc.org
Web site: www.telegraphave.com/gui/awairproductinfo.html

AWAIR provides materials and services for educators teaching about Arabs and Islam for precollege-level educators. It publishes many books and videos, including *The Arab World Notebook, Middle Eastern Muslim Women Speak,* and *Islam.*

Canadian Islamic Congress (CIC)
420 Erb St. West, Suite 424, Waterloo, ON N2L 6K6 Canada

(519) 746-1242

Web site: www.cicnow.com

CIC's stated goals are to establish a national Canadian network of Muslim individuals and organizations; to act in matters affecting the rights and welfare of Canadian Muslims, and to present the interests of Canadian Muslims to Canadian governments, political parties, media, and other organizations.

International Institute of Islamic Thought

PO Box 669, Herndon, VA 20172

(703) 471-1133

e-mail: iiit@iiit.org

Web site: www.iiit.org

This nonprofit academic research facility promotes and coordinates research and related activities in Islamic philosophy, the humanities, and social sciences. It publishes numerous books in both Arabic and English.

Islamic Circle of North America (ICNA)

166-26 Eighty-ninth Ave., Jamaica, NY 11432

(718) 658-1199

e-mail: info@icna.org

Web site: www.icna.org

ICNA works to propagate Islam as a way of life and to establish an Islamic system in North America. It maintains a charitable relief organization and publishes numerous pamphlets in its Islamic Da'wah series as well as the monthly magazine, the *Message.*

Islamic Information Center of America (IICA)

PO Box 4052, Des Plaines, IL 60016

e-mail: iica1@attbi.com

Web site: www.iica.org

IICA is a nonprofit organization that provides information about Islam to Muslims, the general public, and the media. It publishes and distributes a number of pamphlets and a monthly newsletter, the *Invitation.*

Islamic Supreme Council of America (ISCA)

1400 Sixteenth St. NW, Rm. B112, Washington, DC 20036

(202) 939-3400

e-mail: staff@islamicsupremecouncil.org
Web site: www.islamicsupremecouncil.org

The ISCA is a nongovernmental religious organization that promotes Islam in America both by providing practical solutions to American Muslims in integrating Islamic teachings with American culture and by teaching non-Muslims that Islam is a religion of moderation, peace, and tolerance. It strongly condemns Islamic extremists and all forms of terrorism. Its Web site includes statements, commentaries, and reports on terrorism, including "Usama bin Laden: A Legend Gone Wrong" and "Jihad: A Misunderstood Concept from Islam."

Islamic Texts Society
22A Brooklands Ave., Cambridge CB2 2DQ, UK
(44) 1223 314387
e-mail: mail@its.org.uk
Web site: www.its.org.uk

This organization publishes and sells English translations of works of importance to the faith and culture of Islam, with the aim of promoting a greater understanding of Islam. Among the titles it offers is *Understanding Islam and the Muslims*.

Middle East Media Research Institute (MEMRI)
PO Box 27837, Washington, DC 20038-7837
(202) 955-9070
e-mail: memri@erols.com
Web site: www.memri.org

MEMRI translates and disseminates articles and commentaries from Middle East media sources and provides original research and analysis on the region. Its Jihad and Terrorism Studies Project monitors radical Islamist groups and individuals and their reactions to acts of terrorism around the world.

Middle East Policy Council (MEPC)
1730 M St. NW, Suite 512, Washington, DC 20036
(202) 296-6767
e-mail: info@mepc.org
Web site: www.mepc.org

The purpose of this nonprofit organization is to contribute to an understanding of current issues in U.S. relations with countries of the Middle

East. It publishes the quarterly journal *Middle East Policy* as well as special reports and books.

Middle East Studies Association
University of Arizona, 1643 E. Helen St., Tucson, AZ 85721
(520) 621-5850
e-mail: mesana@u.arizona.edu
Web site: http://w3fp.arizona.edu/mesassoc

This professional academic association of scholars on the Middle East focuses particularly on the rise of Islam. It publishes the quarterly *International Journal of Middle East Studies* and runs a project for the evaluation of textbooks for coverage of the Middle East.

Washington Institute for Near East Policy
1828 L St. NW, Washington, DC 20036
(202) 452-0650
e-mail: info@washingtoninstitute.org
Web site: www.washingtoninstitute.org

The institute is an independent, nonprofit research organization that provides information and analysis on the Middle East and U.S. policy in the region. It publishes numerous books, periodic monographs, and reports on regional politics, security, and economics, including *Hezbollah's Vision of the West, Hamas: The Fundamentalist Challenge to the PLO, Democracy and Arab Political Culture, Iran's Challenge to the West, Radical Middle East States and U.S. Policy,* and *Democracy in the Middle East: Defining the Challenge.*

For Further Reading

Books

Ahmed, Akbar S., *Islam Today: A Short Introduction to the Muslim World.* New York: I.B. Tauris, 2001. Explores the conflicting cultural values of the East and West and explains the differences between the Shi'ite and Sunni branches of Islam, women in Islam, and Muslim minorities.

Ansary, Tamin, *West of Kabul, East of New York: An Afghan-American Story.* New York: Farrar, Straus, and Giroux, 2002. A powerful, illuminating memoir that explores a man's journey through the Muslim world. Excellent for young readers.

Armstrong, Karen, *Islam: A Short History.* New York: Modern Library, 2000. An interpretation of Islamic history for a general audience.

Barlas, Asma, *Believing Women in Islam: Unreading Patriarchal Interpretations of the Qu'ran.* Austin: University of Texas Press, 2002. The author argues that the Qur'an actually views women as equal and even superior to men, but misogyny and patriarchy have seeped into Islamic practice through other traditions.

Cook, Michael, *The Koran: A Very Short Introduction.* New York: Oxford University Press, 2000. A useful summary of the origins of the Koran and how it has been used over the last fourteen hundred years.

Esposito, John, *Unholy War: Terror in the Name of Islam.* New York: Oxford University Press, 2002. An expert on contemporary Islam seeks to correct popular misconceptions about the faith. Discusses issues such as the rise of militant Islam and its key personalities.

Haddad, Yvonne Yazbeck, ed., *Muslims in the West: From Sojourners to Citizens.* New York: Oxford University Press, 2002. A collection of essays that look both at the impact of the growing Muslim population on Western societies, and how Muslims are adapting to life in the West.

Hasan, Asama Gull, *American Muslims: The New Generation.* New York: Continuum, 2001. A stimulating look at Islam in the United States written by a young lawyer who is also a self-proclaimed "Muslim feminist cowgirl."

Ibn Warraq, *Why I Am Not a Muslim.* New York: Prometheus, 2003. A former Muslim critically considers the major principles of Islam.

Kepel, Gilles, and Anthony Roberts, *Jihad: The Trail of Political Islam.* Cambridge, MA: Belknap, 2002. A detailed examination of the militant Islamist movement over the last quarter century.

Lewis, Bernard, *The Crisis of Islam: Holy War and Unholy Terror.* New York: Modern Library, 2003. The author explores the sources of Islamic resentment toward the West, especially how the American way of life is a direct threat to Islamic values. He notes that the American way of life—especially that of fulfillment through material gain and sexual freedom—is a direct threat to Islamic values.

Mernissi, Fatima, *Islam and Democracy: Fear of the Modern World.* Cambridge, MA: Perseus, 2002. The author, a Moroccan sociologist, explores the compatibility of Islam and democracy, human rights and religious fundamentalism, from a feminist perspective.

Pipes, Daniel, *Militant Islam Reaches America.* New York: W.W. Norton, 2003. The author, the director of the Middle East Forum, explores the growth of Islamic fundamentalism in the United States.

Ruthven, Malise, *Islam in the World.* 2nd ed. New York: Oxford University Press, 2000. One of the most respected and widely used overviews of Islam.

Spencer, Robert, *Islam Unveiled: Disturbing Questions About the World's Fastest Growing Faith.* San Francisco: Encounter Books, 2002. The author argues that Islam is not a religion of peace and includes evidence of harsh treatment of women and social minorities in Islamic societies.

Weiss, Walter M., *Islam: An Illustrated Historical Overview.* Hauppauge, NY: Barron's, 2000. An entertaining guide to Islam that would be especially useful for a first-time traveler to a Muslim country.

Periodicals

Abowd, Mary, "Ambassadors of Islam," *ColorLines,* Spring 2005.

Africa News Service, "Islam and Gutter Journalism," December 13, 2002.

Akyol, Mustafa, "Islamic Fundamentalism Has More to Do with Hatred of the West than with Religion," *American Enterprise,* April/May 2005.

Alexander, Edward, "Radical Islam vs. Academic Freedom: One Example," *Midstream,* May/June 2002.

Alibhai-Brown, Yasmin, "The Truth About Islam and Women," *Independent* (London, England), October 1, 2001.

Amanullah, Shahed, "'Honor' Killings: Condemnations Are Not Enough," *Alt.Muslim,* December 16, 2002. www.altmuslim.com.

Besançon, Alain, "What Kind of Religion Is Islam?" *Commentary,* May 2004.

Burrell, David B., "The Attraction of Islam: A Community of Faith & Care," *Commonweal,* January 17, 2003.

Butler, Amir, "Political Islam May Yet Be the Answer," *Knight Ridder/Tribune News Service,* May 14, 2003.

Caldwell, Christopher, "Veiled Threat," *Weekly Standard,* January 19, 2004.

Chafets, Zev, "In the Real World, Islam Is a Violent and Aggressive Political Ideology," *Knight Ridder/Tribune News Service,* August 10, 2004.

Dart, John, "Muslims in Motion: The Liberal Side of Islam," *Christian Century,* November 15, 2003.

Dukess, Karen, "Why I Converted to Islam After September 11," *Marie Claire,* June 2002.

Emery, James, "Reputation Is Everything: Honor Killings Among the Palestinians," *World & I,* May 2003.

Fields, Suzanne, "The Many Faces of Islam; Muslims Must Speak Out Against Violence," *Washington Times,* November 4, 2002.

Fox, Frank, "Can Islam Change?" *Liberty,* May 2002.

Furnish, Timothy, "Beheading in the Name of Islam," *Middle East Quarterly,* Spring 2005.

Guppy, Shusha, "Sufism—the Path of Love," *World & I,* July 2003.

Hammad, Aleya El Bindari, "Muslim Women Are the First Victims of Islamic Extremists," *International Herald Tribune,* December 15, 2001.

Haqqani, Husain, "The Rage of Moderate Islam," *Foreign Policy,* January/February 2004.

Hiro, Dilip, "Allah and Democracy Can Get Along Fine," *New York Times,* March 1, 2005.

Hymowitz, Kay S., "Why Feminism Is AWOL on Islam," *City Journal,* Winter 2003.

Jatras, James George, "Is There a *Khilafah* in Your Future? The Coming Islamic Revolution," *Chronicles,* February 2005.

Khan, Hiraa Amber, "Peaceful Muslims Deserve Better," *America's Intelligence Wire,* October 21, 2004.

Kinabalu, Kota, "Western Media Not Helpful in Correcting Perception of Islam," *Asia Africa Intelligence Wire,* March 28, 2005.

Kremmer, Janaki, "Taking a Stand for Moderate Islam," *Christian Science Monitor,* July 21, 2004.

Leggett, Karby, "Women Win New Rights in Morocco by Invoking Islam," *Wall Street Journal,* August 10, 2004.

Malik, Mustafa, "Seeds of Hate: How America's Flawed Middle East Policy Ignited the Jihad," *Middle East Policy,* Summer 2004.

Marayati Laila al-, and Semeen Issa, "An Identity Reduced to a Burka," *Los Angeles Times,* January 20, 2002.

Mekouar, Aziz, "Islam and Democracy; Morocco Shows the Way," *Washington Times,* March 15, 2004.

Muhaisen, Wadi, "America's Shameful Mideast History," *Rocky Mountain News,* November 22, 2002.

an-Na'im, Abdullahi, "Islam and Human Rights," *Tikkun,* January/February 2003.

Pollitt, Katha, "As Miss World Turns," *Nation,* December 23, 2002.

Sardar, Ziauddin, "Muslim World: A Choice Between Saudi and Turkey," *New Statesman,* March 22, 2004.

Scruton, Rojer, "Religion of Peace? Islam, Without the Comforting Clichés," *National Review,* December 31, 2002.

Stack, Megan K., "The Many Layers of the Veil," *Los Angeles Times,* January 12, 2005.

Steyn, Mark, "We Still Don't Get It," *Spectator,* September 11, 2004.

Tammeus, Bill, "Moderate Muslims Must Reassert Control over Islam," *Kansas City Star,* July 5, 2002.

Tate, Sonsyrea, "In Defense of Islam; Young Muslim Women Must Fight for Change," *Washington Times,* May 9, 2002.

Vincent, Steven, "Where Are the Moderate Muslims?" *American Enterprise,* April/May 2005.

West, Diana, "Preserve Free Speech: Journalists Afraid to Criticize Islam," *Washington Times,* April 8, 2005.

Wilson, James Q., "Islam and Freedom," *Commentary,* December 2004.

Yahya, Harun, "The Eminence Islam Attaches to Women," *Muslim Women's League,* www.mwlusa.org.

Web Sites

American Muslim Council (http://www.amcnational.org). Founded in 1990, this organization seeks to increase the political participation of Muslim Americans. The Web site has the group's history, current projects, news releases, and links to more than three dozen other Islamic Web sites.

Council on American-Islamic Relations (www.cair-net.org). A nonprofit organization that works with journalists and others to improve the image of Islam and Muslims. The Web site contains news releases, action alerts, and information on how the media portray Islam.

Islam.com (www.islam.com). A comprehensive site with information and articles on how to practice Islam, Islamic texts, holidays and festivals, and community issues.

Muslim Public Affairs Council (www.mpac.org). Since 1988, the council has organized numerous meetings between Muslim leaders and political candidates and elected officials. It also works closely with similar organizations representing other ethnic and religious groups. The Web site contains information on the group's activities and suggestions for political involvement.

Talk Islam (www.talkislam.com). A Web site with links to hundreds of Islamic organizations and Internet documents.

Index